SUSSEX FOLK AND SUSSEX WAYS

A Sussex Veteran wearing Embroidered "Gaberdine"

SUSSEX FOLK AND SUSSEX WAYS

BY THE LATE
JOHN COKER EGERTON, M.A.

RECTOR OF BURWASH 1867–1888

EDITED BY THE LATE
HENRY WACE, D.D.

DEAN OF CANTERBURY

WITH A NEW PREFACE BY
SHEILA KAYE-SMITH

CLXX

NEW EDITION
WITH EIGHT ILLUSTRATIONS

METHUEN & CO. LTD.
36 ESSEX STREET W.C.
LONDON

Originally Published by Messrs. Chatto & Windus in 1892
First Published (Third Edition, Revised) by
Methuen & Co., Ltd., in 1924

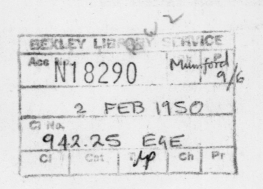
PRINTED IN GREAT BRITAIN

CONTENTS

LIST OF ILLUSTRATIONS

AN INTRODUCTION
TO THE PRESENT EDITION

BY

SHEILA KAYE-SMITH

" To love and to cherish,
   From Battle to Berrish,
   And round about Robertsbridge home. . . ."

SO runs the old marriage-rhyme of the upper
Rother. Berrish—or perhaps more strictly Bur-
rish—is the Rev. John Coker Egerton's parish
according to local pronunciation, or rather according
to the local pronunciation of a by-gone day. For
Sussex people are learning from London how to pro-
nounce their own names. Londoners have driven
lovely Horse-ham into banal Horsham, they have in
their ignorance Scotchified Ber-wick into Berrick, and
contrariwise, drawled out Berrish into Burwash. And
who in Heathfield's three-mile street still speaks of
Heffle Fair ?

It is not only the names that have changed. Mr.
Egerton's prophecy at the beginning of his book has
already been fulfilled. " In a few years' time the
manners and customs of Sussex men, women and children will have passed away as utterly as pack-horses
and stage wagons. ' Round frocks ' will be extinct,

and with them the characteristics of mind, thought
and speech which round frocks betokened. I well
know that the change must come, but I own that I
look forward with but little satisfaction to the time
when our boys and girls will all speak a uniform
language prescribed by the Committee of Council
on Education, and when our men and women will
think only just as other people think."

No doubt this is true. From the point of charm,
quaintness, beauty and originality, Sussex, like every
other county in England, has changed for the worse.
But one cannot wish the old times back, for all their
" round frocks," racy speech and original manners.
For they were bad old times—times of poverty and
squalor, of hunger and injustice and ill-rewarded
labour. The misery of the agricultural classes dates
from the end of the Middle Ages. No doubt they
suffered under feudalism, which compared badly with
the Saxon democracy of the land, but the ill-usage of
feudalism was like the ill-usage of a capricious parent,
and its abuses lay in the individual rather than in the
system. The ill-usage of the post-Reformation landlord, enriched with Abbey lands, and the Elizabethan
poor-law which took the place of the Abbey's charity,
was the cast-iron ill-usage of an institution, and its
abuses lay in the system itself rather than in its
administrators.

During the sixteenth and seventeenth centuries the
field-labourer came more and more to be ignored by
the nation at large ; he was finally lost in a haze of
sentimental neglect, as the power of the Hanoverian
landlords grew side by side with the " picturesque "
convention of the Hanoverian poets. Then came the
dark days before the Repeal of the Corn Laws, the

" Hungry Forties," when wages were sixpence a day and mothers sent their children out into the fields at dark to steal turnips for the empty pot. . . . Even when the labouring man was given a political Voice, and received, in consequence, some small consideration, his progress was still slow. In this book Mr. Egerton reproduces the pathetic little budget of the housewife who " managed " for herself, her husband and six children, on 15s. 6d. a week; and I have heard of a labourer's wife who did the same for eleven children on as many shillings.

No, we would not wish the old times back, though the new have much to be said against them too, and the loss of individuality seems a heavy price to pay for a mediocre prosperity and a mediocre education. Sussex is becoming more and more Londonized. Not only are our local names being changed for us by the once-despised " furriner," but the racy Sussex dialect, with its affinity with real English as spoken in America, and its survival of Saxon and Norman words, is crumbling away before the advancing tide of Cockney. In a household of three generations you will get three different kinds of speech. Ask Grandfather if it will be a stormy day and he will tell you, " Surelye, fur de ships' tails is all to wind'ard." Father will answer, " Well, it may be, for the glass is low," while Sonny will reply, " Not half." He hasn't got so far as " Not arf " yet, but that is surely coming.

At a certain inn on the Kentish border the landlord's wife owns to spending £250 a year on her clothes. This would be a strange tale in the days of Mr. Egerton's " Labour in Vain "; but it does not mean that the country is particularly prosperous, though conditions are certainly not so bad as they were in, for instance, the year 1830, " when the annual loss on farming operations within the parish was £15,488 17s. 6d." Improved methods of cultivation, and the rise of the big seaside towns with their markets for fruit and vegetables and poultry, have no doubt improved the farmer's lot, though he still struggles with labour difficulties and heavy rates.   Grain and hops no longer pay, and the future seems to lie in live-stock.

Both farmer and farm-labourer are suffering from the reaction following the wave of prosperity that swept agricultural districts during the war.   The removal of Government guarantees makes it impossible for the farmer to pay anything like the wages he paid in those record years, and naturally the worker does not appreciate the change.   Personally, I should say that salvation lies in the small landlord ; and with the collapse of the big estates and the tradition of the squires, the peasant landowner seems at least a possibility.   But we have to contend also with a growing dissatisfaction with country life, a shrinking from the monotony and isolation inseparable from it.   The linking together of country villages by enterprising motor-bus services may help us here—it is already breaking down the loneliness of many farms ; and I should like to say a word for the despised " pictures," which can make a place of education and entertainment of many a village hall, hitherto given over to " penny readings " and painful recitations.   I have no sympathy with the idea that country people should be content with utter monotony and dullness, and indeed we shall find it to our advantage if we make agriculture more attractive to educated and lively young people, though side by side with the Cinema, I would put in a plea for the revival of the joyful old customs which are peculiarly and hereditarily rural—the May Day festival, the Harvest Home, the Wake, the Fair.

But fortunately my concern here is not with the future but with the past—the past of fifty years ago which seems so particularly far away. Fifty years ago, when the Rev. John Coker Egerton was Rector of Burwash, my father was doctor at Battle. He talked often of those Battle days, of the " rounds " on horse-back—three horses working in relays, so that the beast might have the rest which was impossible to the man . . . of operations carried out in some cottage bed-room, by the light of a candle held by the labourer's wife . . . of adventures in roads made impassable by snow and darkness. I still have his road map, and use it in sentimental preference to more modern pro-ductions, though many a time it has betrayed my car into a nearly impassable lane, or sent me circuiting through by-ways, ignorant of the new macadam be-tween me and my goal.

There is an indirect reference to my father in Mr. Egerton's record, when he mentions the typhoid epidemic which was traced to its ignominious source in the milkman's well. Many a time have I heard the story of that epidemic and how it threatened, even after the discovery of its origin, to sweep the whole village. My father attributed its ending to a terrific thunderstorm which " washed the place clean."

Mr. Egerton's record drifts along in a stream of anecdotes, rather casually grouped under subjects, such as school, church, roads, farm-life, etc.—from which, nevertheless, there soon emerges quite a definite little world, the little world of a Sussex village in the nineteenth century, with many of its old ways still surviving and its new ways just begun. The personality of the author, with his human kindness and diffidence, is a pleasing quality of the stories he tells. He seems to have been especially fitted for his vocation as shepherd of Sussex sheep, and his flock seem to have admitted him to fellowship with a readiness which is the greatest tribute the slow Sussex man can pay the " furriner," who whether he come as Parson or Doctor often remains a " furriner " till the end.

Personally the part of the book which interests me most is the " Lecture on the History of Burwash " at the end. Unlike Mr. Egerton, who says that " though I have lived nearly the whole of my life in the country, country human nature is almost my only country taste," I have always felt drawn to the elusive, mysterious personality of places. I am interested in their history as I am interested in a friend's past life, and I should like above all things to have a library consisting entirely of Sussex Parish Histories, a volume to each place, after the manner of Mr. Leonard Hodson's " Salehurst " and " Udimore."

Just as one wants to know the pasts of some people more than others, simply because they look interesting at their present age, so I am specially glad to know how Burwash grew on the Hill above the Swamp. To-day its shady street runs along the ridge between two valleys, one shallow and marshy, the valley of Etchingham and the Rother, with Ticehurst and Wadhurst, and Hurst Green (the villages of the woods) on the hills beyond it ; the other steep and choked with little fields, the valley of the Dudwell, lying at the foot of the great hill which is sharp with the point of Brightling Needle. The roads that wander round Burwash are very different now from the days when ruts and mud made wheel-traffic almost impossible. Now one of the best roads in the district runs " from Battle to Berrish, and round about Robertsbridge home." The population has increased, though not so terrifyingly as at Battle, where a gruesome " new town " has been conjured up by the black magic of the Ministry of Health. But even so, two dreary rows of bright red-brick cottages spoil the lovely slope between Burwash and the Rother. I have watched them for years in the hope that they were going to fade, but their bricks and tiles remain " still untouch'd by time's rude hand."

Mr. Kipling with his sure sense of locality and nomenclature employs some of the old traditional names in his two Burwash-born books, " Puck of Pook's Hill " and " Rewards and Fairies," in which an older Burwash than even Mr. Egerton loved is magically brought to light. For Mr. Kipling of " Bateman's " has now, for some years, been the most illustrious inhabitant of the countryside.

It is good to find many of the old names lingering in the neighbourhood. Cramps and Cruttendens are still to be found, though Mr. Egerton tells us the last Cruttenden was gone from the parish itself fifty years ago. Indeed, in the matter of family names, Sussex does not share the dispersal of Surrey, and one may see at least some of the old names in the old places—little nests of Ponts by Three Cups Corner and Punnett's Town, Fullers at Brightling, and Vidlers at Rye. Mostly these are humble survivors. Cottagers in the wilds of Ashburnham can point to coats of arms they have the right to bear.

Mr. Egerton's book brings the old times sufficiently near to us for us to see how much in them we are glad is gone, and how much in them we should be sorry to lose. " Doubtless hereafter Sussex folk will be superior to their grandfathers in knowledge and exact science —they will possibly also earn more money, and they will live better. I pray that they may be happier also, and that together with better times, honesty and good faith between man and man may also increase and abound, and such honourable doctrines as a fair day's work for a fair day's wage, as well as a fair day's wage for a fair day's work, may not perish with all the picturesqueness of our Sussex life in the olden times."

PREFACE TO THE SECOND EDITION

BY

THE LATE PREBENDARY HARRY JONES

I HAVE been asked to write a preface to the present edition of this little book. My first impulse is to evade the request, not because I fail to realize its worth, but lest (however short the overture) I should strike a misleading note. Some will make merry over the procession of stories which the author leads through his pages, and call him "entertaining." A poor verdict. Others, looking a little deeper, will see suggestive pictures of village life, and graphic records of expiring traditions. But as more read what is here written, they will, I think, perceive that its memorials of local history and vanishing legends, its anecdotes, and nuggets of genial wisdom, come from the pen of one who had eyes to see, rather than views to impart. He possessed that undefinable power of perception which looks into the heart of a thing or man without missing any of its or his outward and visible features. And he exercised this in a tenderly genuine Christian spirit, accompanied by that latent sense of vital humour, which not only distinguishes between real wit and ridiculous claims, but pricks bubbles with discriminate confidence, and altogether refuses to be imposed upon.

If the readers of this volume do not take it up again and again, after first laying it down, to find more worth reading and thinking about each time, nothing that I, or anyone else, could write in the way of a preface would serve as a fit introduction to that which it contains. So I wipe my pen with the comfortable thought that (whether prefaced by a few friendly lines or not) another edition of " Sussex Folk and Sussex Ways " is being put into the hands of such as can appreciate wisdom, humour, and valuable contributions to the store of those records which tell us of English rustic life.

IN MEMORIAM—
JOHN COKER EGERTON [1]

A VERY large circle of friends will have been grieved by the announcement of the death, on the 19th of last month, of the Rev. John Coker Egerton, rector of Burwash, in Sussex. He was only fifty-eight years of age, in the prime of ministerial efficiency, and his death, probably due to some cardiac failure, fell as an almost sudden blow upon his parishioners. He was in many ways a man of rare excellence and usefulness, and exercised a singularly varied influence for good. His characteristic natural gift was perhaps that of kindly sympathy with men of all classes and ages; and this faculty was employed, under the impulse of a simple and devout piety, in a constant effort to promote true religion and good living among all with whom he was associated. His abilities enabled him to enter with interest into the varied developments of thought and action in his day, and he found some point of contact with almost every one whom he met. He retained to the last the tincture of classical scholarship which he gained at Shrewsbury under Dr. Kennedy. At Oxford he took a Third Class in *Literæ Humaniores* in 1852, and became one of the Hulme Exhibitioners of Brasenose. He rowed in his college boat in the palmy days of Brasenose on the river; and to the last

---

[1] From the " Guardian," April 18, 1888.

the Brasenose boat and good oarsmanship, " with the turn good rowing gives, sirs " (as he said in some lines he wrote), had a strong hold on his interests and even affections. It was his delight to maintain genial and friendly relations with each successive college crew, and until the University associations of the Oxford and Cambridge race had been lost in the excitement of a metropolitan holiday he was similarly constant in his devotion to successive Oxford crews. His genial company and his humorous stories were welcome in all societies, and especially among young men ; and he helped to carry on from generation to generation some of the best traditions of Oxford life.

But this inherent capacity of sympathy found its special sphere in the work of a country clergyman. He served his first curacy at Nunton, near Salisbury, from 1854 to 1857 ; he was then curate of Burwash from 1857 to 1862 ; and, after a change for three years to a London curacy at St. Andrew Undershaft, in the City, he returned to Burwash to serve again as curate until 1867. He then became rector, and held the living till his death. He thus held ministerial charge in Burwash for nearly thirty years, and in the course of that time he had established an affectionate and even devoted confidence between himself and his parishioners, which received most striking expression on his death. Numbers of them begged to be allowed to see him again in his coffin, and he almost lay in state like an emperor— or rather like a friend. The secret of this affection for him lay in his singular power of sympathy for every individual and every feeling, combined with a perfectly simple and natural faithfulness to his duty in all circumstances of his intercourse with his people. He understood their special characters, their humours, their weaknesses, and their strength ; he entered into every detail of their daily occupations ; and all the while, as they were sensible, he was trying to help them to fight the same battle as he was fighting himself, against the various religious and moral temptations which both he and they experienced.

Though, of course, he knew his Sussex folk best, he had shown the same capacity wherever his work had been cast. He paid regular annual visits to his first parish near Salisbury, and during his three years in London he established relations of affection and confidence with poor parishioners, which were never broken. His sympathetic enjoyment of the peculiar qualities of his Sussex people is exhibited in a charming volume, published by Trübner in 1884, entitled " Sussex Folk and Sussex Ways ; or, Stray Studies in the Wealden Formation of Human Nature," and this genial record of Sussex humour is equally characteristic of the writer and of his " Sussex folk." But he could be similarly sympathetic with scholars and men in higher positions, and there are some among them who owe him a deep debt of gratitude for the support he rendered them, in anxious crises of their lives, by his simple and pious, while thoughtful, faith. He acted, in fact, very much as a mediator between the current thought of his age and the humble life and simple necessities of it. His country sermons showed that he understood the doubts and difficulties which, though mainly felt in the great centres of thought, yet, as he knew, are apt, in these days of a cheap press, to cast their shadows even over country life ; and though it requires great discretion to notice such difficulties before a simple congregation, it may be a protection to many minds to feel that their teacher is not unaware of the new movements of thought around them. On the other hand, he could bring to his more cultivated friends, in town and country, a sense of the real and permanent necessities of daily life and death, and thus steady their speculations by a sympathetic apprehension of practical realities. Music exercised a great influence on his life, and through him on the lives of others. It was the one relaxation he allowed himself in his work : but as years passed on, he had rarely time even for this ; though his intense love of what he termed the " one pure art " grew stronger rather than otherwise. In a word, he was a true man, a true Christian, and a true friend, with a rare gift of sympathy, which brought home to all around him the truth of his nature and his faith. It is a mysterious dispensation which removes him, in the prime of his influence, from the parish in which he was such a centre of all good influences, and from the wife and five young children, with whom he lived a life of rare domestic happiness. But it is eminently true of him that he " had fought a good fight, and had kept the faith " ; and so far as he is concerned it can be no matter of lament that he has finished his course here.

HENRY WACE

P.S. (written in 1923 in a letter from Dean Wace to Mrs. Coker Egerton) :

" I am thankful that the book is alive, and is to enter on a new spell of life. I congratulate you warmly on the prospect it opens for the further influence of the book and for the due recognition of the author's life and work. That such a revival should be possible after more than thirty years is a very remarkable tribute to the book and its author."

SUSSEX FOLK AND SUSSEX WAYS

I

THOUGH I have lived nearly the whole of my life in the country, country human nature is almost my only country taste. I am ashamed to own that I know hardly anything about the lives and habits of the birds, beasts, and fishes which are to be found in my parish. Trees, ferns, and wild flowers afford me a real but sadly unscientific enjoyment; and with the geological formation of the district I have but a very superficial acquaintance, derived mainly from the various kinds of mud which I encounter in my parochial walks. With country people, however, I have a keen sympathy. Their habits of thought, their opinions, their prejudices, their superstitions, their manner of speech, their quaint expressions, their dry humour, their shrewd sense, their civilities, and even their harmless rudeness, have an interest for me which makes my country life a very happy one. Sussex human nature has afforded me the most opportunities of observation, inasmuch as I have spent nearly all my clerical life in a large and somewhat wild parish in the Eastern division of that county; and my belief in the various good qualities of East Sussex human nature, after making full allowance for all drawbacks, is thoroughly sincere.

In its outward manifestations, however, it is undergoing such a rapid change, that in a few years' time the manners and customs of Sussex men, women, and children with whom I have long been familiar, will have passed away as utterly as pack-horses and stage wagons. " Round frocks " will be extinct, and with them the characteristics of mind, thought, and speech which round frocks betokened. I well know that the change must come, but I own that I look forward with little satisfaction to the time when our boys and girls will all speak a uniform language prescribed by the Committee of Council on Education, and when our men and women will think only just as other people think.

At present, racy Saxon speech, which gains in force much that it may lose in elegance, is still to be heard among us, and premises which have been leisurely " draaed through " our native minds, yield conclusions quite as reasonable as those reached by more professed thinkers, and conclusions at times far more originally expressed.

Many years ago I heard from a parishioner an opinion of politics, which, whoever was its author, had in my ears a true Sussex ring about it, and which I felt to be no mere second-hand cynicism, but the genuine belief, however much mistaken, of some dweller in the country, who, thinking for himself, had come to doubt the existence of political honesty.

" Well," he said, " in my opinion, politics are about like this : I've got a sow in my yard with twelve little uns, and they little uns can't all feed at once, because there isn't room enough, so I shut six on 'em out of the yard while t'other six be sucking, and the six as be shut out, they just do make a hem of a noise till they be let in, and then they be just as quiet as the rest."

I have heard another parishioner expressing himself much to the same effect, when he used to say—

" I be a miller, and I've got rats, and I keep cats, and one day I looks into a place under my mill, and there I sees cats and rats all feeding together out of one trough at my expense."

Whether these reflections are true or not, is quite another matter, but I believe them to be opinions formed independently, and not the echoes of the Clubs or newspapers.

This particular difficulty in believing in political honesty is, however, not confined to our county, for one of my Sussex neighbours tells me that a friend canvassing in a Metropolitan borough at the last election, was met by this objection, that it mattered little who went to Parliament, for that they all made a lot of money by it. In vain was it urged that it was just the other way, that a seat in " The House " meant money out of pocket instead of in.

" Come," said the voter, " I'm not going to believe that. Don't you see in the paper often enough, cries of ' Divide ! Divide ! ' Now, do you think they'd cry ' Divide ! Divide ! ' if they'd got nothin' to divide ? No, no ! they just take the taxes and divide them amongst themselves—that's what they do."

I myself, though no politician, once fell under an amusing suspicion in the matter of money on the part of some of my flock. When I married, my parishioners were kind enough to make me a handsome present— the result of a parochial subscription. Some time afterwards I was reminded of the fact, by being told of an unexpected criticism which was current, viz. that it was " a curious thing that our parson couldn't get married without sending the hat round for money to pay his wedding expenses."

The moral which I deduced was an additional argument for the necessity of disarming suspicion by the utmost publicity in, at any rate, all money matters in which one is in any sense a trustee for the parish. Nor is suspicion on the part of our poor limited either to politics or to parsons. I was told the other day that on some of the best " canned " meats being shown to a poor woman in the village shop in the next parish to ours, she promptly replied—

" No, no ; none of them things for me ; they be all lions and unicorns—they be."

The good body might well be excused doubting the tenderness of such meat. An old Sussex working ox was never looked upon as furnishing the choicest joints, but, as compared with lions and unicorns, it would probably be tenderness itself.

Who, again, can find fault with the incredulity of a west-country cottager of whom I heard many years ago, that, in speaking to a district visitor, or to a " 'strict lady," as I have heard a district visitor called among ourselves, she said—

" Ah, ma'am, my son that has been up to the North Pole, he tells me some things that I really can't believe, though he is my son. He tells me, ma'am, that he has seen with his own eyes ' ice bugs ' as big as a church."

It is not easy to realize the claim which such an assertion would make upon the faith of a cleanly old English countrywoman. What, too, could be more natural than the wonderment of a poor man, one of my Wiltshire flock, who, having been to see the Great Exhibition in 1851, returned with this one overwhelming difficulty in his mind, " How the gentlefolks could like to eat ' Poor Man's Friend,' " a well-known red ointment, very similar in colour and consistency to the raspberry ices which he saw largely consumed, and which in his innocence he took for the, to him, much more familiar but nauseous compound. But to return to Sussex.

Our people live much by themselves, and they think for themselves, and their judgments of men and things are often delightfully fresh and unconventional.

It was not, however, one of my own people, but an inhabitant of the more enlightened borough of Lewes, who, being asked after a general election how he had given his vote, replied—

" Well, I've voted for the Tories ever so long, but this time I thought I'd give these Conservatives a turn ! "

Personally, I have little reason to look upon Sussex politics with satisfaction ; my experience of them having been a trying one. I was once voting for the county, and though it is true that the opinions which I upheld were successful, I suffered much every way in giving effect to them at the poll. The arrangements at Mayfield were such that I was crushed as badly as I ever was in a London crowd, and I escaped at last from the schoolroom in which the votes were taken, only to be encountered by a more than half-drunken voter, whose unhappy memory served him to reproduce for my benefit one, I think, of Cobbett's irreverent sayings, which he bellowed out from the opposite side of the street—

" My politics be these : I be for more fat pigs and less fat parsons."

Apropos of pigs,

" Some men there are love not a gaping pig."
Merchant of Venice, iv. I.

I am of Shakespeare's mind on this point, and I almost wonder that I can look one in the face, as I associate them chiefly with ideas of rebuke and indignity. Soon after I came into Sussex, a neighbouring clergyman gave me a splendid mastiff as a companion in my walks. That it could draw upon me a reference to the unclean animal any more than to parrots or porcupines, was an idea that had not entered into my head. However, so it was ; over and over again had I to listen to the vexatiously practical formula—

" Excuse me, sir, but, in my humble way of thinking, it would pay you a deal better to keep a couple of pigs."

Poor Mona ! how I hated pork when I thought of her stately uselessness, and felt that, in my people's eyes, she ought to be represented by two of the least lovable creatures upon earth ! But my cup of humiliation in connection with pigs was not yet full, and it remained for a poor man at Bournemouth to fill it. I was admiring one evening a very fine donkey which was standing outside the Highcliffe Mansions Hotel in a cart in which was a hog-tub. While I was listening to the praises of the animal's temper and speed, which its owner began to pour out very freely, his mate came out from the hotel with a pail of wash. This he emptied into the tub, and then, seeing me talking to the man with the donkey, and taking me for the proprietor of the hotel, to whom he evidently wished to speak, he came up to me and said—

" Please, sir, are you the gen'lman as belongs to the wash ? "

Now, if the wash had belonged to me it would not have conferred any great dignity upon me, and I own that, on the contrary, to be addressed as a mere adjunct to the wash, as a mere complement of a hog-tub, confirmed me in my abhorrence of pigs and all that belongs to them. And yet I have heard a crest and a motto derived from this very animal, attributed to our county, pointing to a temper which may be either simple obstinacy or that honourable sturdiness of resistance to pressure, whether in matters of opinion or of practice, which in England produces " Village Hampdens," and, fortunately, when occasions need, national ones also. Our crest, it is said, is " a hog," and our motto, " We wun't be druv." Be this as it may, it seems to me perfectly true that mere authority goes but a little way with a genuine Sussex man.

> " If reasons were as plenty as blackberries,
> I would give no man a reason on compulsion."
>> *Henry IV*, ii. 4.

This impatience of compulsion enabled one of my parishioners, fifty years ago, as I am told, to maintain a long and successful resistance even to the combined influence of his wife and every member of his family. The good man was the owner of an enormous hog, which had grown so coarse and unpleasant, that when it was killed all in the house declined to touch it, and insisted that it should be buried. This peremptory request put the good man so completely on his mettle, that he then and there registered a vow, that sooner than bury the hog he would eat it himself, and as my informant assured me, he used to say, " I kept my word, though I was two years about it." The truth of this tradition having been unkindly questioned, I have taken some pains to verify it. I confess with regret that the history of the particular hog to which the story was attached I have traced, by aid of the memory of one of our old people, to a different and more commonplace end. Still, the account was so circumstantially given by the contemporary curate of Burwash, since, alas! dead, that I feel fairly confident that as regards some hog or other the tradition is true.

Again, I have known a Sussex man give up his cottage and subject himself to some expense and much inconvenience rather than sacrifice the life of a favourite cat which was suspected of poaching.

" No," said the man, not unreasonably, " if they'd catch'd him at it, that would be another thing altogether, but I'm not goin' to have my cat killed naun the more just because they ' think ' he poaches."

An amusing instance of our independence, though based, I fear, on arrant selfishness, occurred many years ago, so I have heard, when the Prince of Wales, afterwards George IV, happened to be passing through the village on his return to Brighton from a visit to Sir John Ladd, one of his Royal Highness's boon companions, who was then staying in the adjoining parish of Etchingham.

Our bells were not rung, and for our lack of loyalty we fell under the royal displeasure. Inquiry was made, and the reason alleged by the ringers for their silence was, that—

" They had rung for him when he came thro' the

first time, and he gave them no beer, so they weren't going to ring for him again ; not likely ! "

Strangers who have bought property in the parish have often been greatly struck by the " fore-rightness " and impatience of anything approaching to high-handed treatment exhibited by our working men. I well remember the conclusion to which a retired officer of the army soon came who had bought one of our farms, and who found that orders given in barrack-yard tone were not received with exactly barrack-yard submission. He honestly avowed that he would far sooner command a regiment of soldiers than one Burwash labourer. Another new proprietor, who is long since dead, but whose temper and language while he was with us were not quite such as accorded with our views of what is due from an employer to those whom he employs, speedily received from one of his labourers the following assurance.

" You see, sir, it's like this. If you was to go on at me for about five minutes as you go on at your gardener, we should part."

I have known even a kind suggestion resented, only because the recipient fancied he detected a tone of patronage and authority in what was said. One bitter winter morning, one of my parishioners overtook a cart in which was a boy who had got a lift. The poor boy looked so miserably cold that my good friend said to him compassionately—

" If I were you, my little man, I'd get down and walk."

" No, that I wun't ; not if I freeze fust," was the indignant reply.

Surely there was, at any rate, a tenacity of purpose in that boy which ought in some way or other to

stand its possessor in good stead, and I have often
been sorry that I have lost sight of the lad.   One old
man I knew well in my early Sussex days, of whom
it was said that he boasted that " he had never bent
his knee to any man." But in this case it must be
admitted that he had a " straight knee," and could
not bend it at all.   It must not, however, be supposed
that our native population are not amenable to any
discipline.   They are, on the contrary, very tractable
if they are approached in the right way, but the mere
exercise of authority is perhaps the least successful
method of dealing with them.

In our depressed times, a good many years ago, one
of our able-bodied parishioners was an inmate of the
workhouse, and feeling, I suppose, aggrieved by being
obliged to go into " the house," he showed his feelings
from time to time by various acts of insubordination.
For these he was necessarily punished, and I have
always understood that he accepted his fate with the
dogged remark—

" Well, gentlemen, as long as you choose to find
punishment, I'll find back."

The man certainly was not one of our finer spirits,
and passed among us as somewhat ill-conditioned ;
still, submit quietly he would not to a power which
he considered to be unjustly exercised.

Another more light-hearted, but far more culpable
offender, used to be credited with an enviable equa-
nimity, produced by simply balancing what he had
deserved against what he had got. " I don't know,"
he used to say, " that I have any call to complain.
I've been to Lewes six times ; three times they found
me guilty when I hadn't done nothin', and three times
they let me off when I was guilty." So long as he

could feel, even by the aid of his imperfect logic, that on the whole he had had justice done him, he was content. " Oppression makes the wise man mad," says Solomon ; and whether our people are wise or not, I cannot help feeling that the Saxon spirit of resistance to whatever may even savour of oppression has survived in a somewhat greater degree than usual among the East Sussex peasantry with whom I am best acquainted, and that it makes them, in their own phrase, " mad " more readily than it does some of the more phlegmatic of their countrymen.

To me, the sense of living among people who are not afraid to speak their mind and let me know their real sentiments is most satisfactory, and I may add that my theory on this point was, in a small matter, once put to a curiously practical test. I had been giving a lecture in the schoolroom on " The Characteristics of an Englishman," and I had, I suppose, put rather prominently forward an Englishman's natural love of independence, and of doing as he likes. At any rate, as I came away from the lecture, I profited, I hope, by the independent criticism of one of my younger hearers, " Well, I was an Englishman ; I did as I liked ; I went to sleep." I am glad to say that my faith in my own doctrine did not fail me, and that I value this testimony far more than I should have done the insipid generality, " Oh, yes, sir, it were all very nice."

This spirit of independence and " fore-rightness," if sometimes rather too strongly developed, has, at any rate, I think, one good effect—it tends to take hypocrisy out of the number of our besetting sins. Hypocrisy, I fancy, meets with scant sympathy in the minds of our Sussex folk. There is plenty of it, no doubt, but the public conscience, I believe, abhors it, however successfully some of our less scrupulous brethren may practise it.   There is possibly, I fear, a touch of selfishness in this general condemnation of a hypocrite, inasmuch as I commonly hear one very strong reason urged for the indignation—viz. that when hypocrisy is found out, as, sooner or later, in our limited community it almost always is, it makes kind-hearted people suspicious, and so dries up the stream of liberality which would otherwise have continued to flow.   Still, apart from this, there is among us, I am sure, a keen sense of the shamefulness of imposing upon good nature, and a skilful hypocrite must not expect to enjoy his success amid the applause of admiring neighbours.   Once, when asking in a lesson in school the meaning of the word " hypocrite," I got the following pertinent answer : " When a man walks lame as hasn't got nothin' the matter wi' him " ; but whatever the definition of hypocrisy may be, the thing itself is well understood, and as a rule heartily detested.   I once met with a curious instance of the feeling of indignation at the accusation of hypocrisy in the person of an old man, one of my parishioners, who, being in " the union," was out for a holiday.   I was asking him how he got on in " the house," which I was sure was the best place for him, seeing that he was in years, was infirm, and not very strong-minded. He spoke fairly contentedly of his lot, but one thing evidently rankled in his mind, for he stopped, and, leaning on the two " bats," i.e. sticks, with which he was walking, said, rather excitedly, " The master calls me a hypocrip—he does.   Now," he said, " if I be a hypocrip "—and an impediment in his speech, made worse by his excitement, caused him to stutter terribly

as he spoke—" I wish somebody would take one of
these bub-bub-bats, and hide me bub-bub-bang out."
He could not well have expressed himself more forcibly.

On the whole, then, I think I may say with confidence, that anyone coming to live among us, and studying the character of our people, would be favourably
impressed with our freedom of thought and speech,
as well as by the quaint forms which that thought
and speech occasionally take.

II

TO an outside observer, the main feature of the life of our peasantry is probably its seemingly sad monotonous dulness. Our ideas of enjoyment would not unlikely be looked upon as being fairly represented by the following theory of a holiday, which, five and twenty years ago, a Sussex friend told me was carried almost literally into practice in an adjoining parish. Master Wimber having determined to take a day's holiday after twenty years' hard work, was puzzling his brains all the night before as to what he should do with his holiday when he got it. His wife and himself had sat over the fire for a couple of hours debating the question, but to no purpose, when a bright idea struck him, and he was at once clear in his mind. He would buy four ounces of " 'baccer," and sit on the " mixen " and smoke it out.

Again, what could be a sadder form of amusement than one which revealed itself some time since in answer to the master of our national school, who asked a boy how he had come by a great scratch all down the side of his face ?

" Please, sir, we were playing at pig-killing," was the reply, " and he had to kill me, and he did it with his knife."

Without doubt our country life at times is very dull. I was once sharply reminded of the fact by a talk which I had with a boy about nine years old, who had

AN AGED BURWASH COUPLE, 1888

come down from London to see some relations. Among other questions, I happened to ask him whether he liked the country, and finding that he was by no means enthusiastic in its praise, I pressed him for some reason for his indifference, when he answered very decidedly—

" There ain't no society."

I was a little taken aback, I confess, by the *ennui* of this little man of the world, but it seemed to show very forcibly the way in which our quiet existence strikes persons who are used even to the mere physical excitement of town life.

I am, however, strongly inclined to think that we are not so dull as people give us credit for being. We have a certain amount of humour among us, and minds that are really capable of humour must, I imagine, have some fund of native cheerfulness which is independent of excitement. Indeed, my experience of a London curacy would lead me to suppose that the life of a family which is one of six or seven in the same house is by no means necessarily more cheerful than the life of a family occupying one of our cottages in the fields. The part which humour plays in our daily country life is, I am persuaded, a more important one than is commonly supposed. A good saying, a rustically clever repartee, a hearty joke with a sufficiently broad and palpable point, lasts us a long time, is handed about, is thoroughly appreciated, secures from time to time a good honest laugh, and has much the same effect among us as the latest *bon mot* of some acknowledged wit has on a Parisian public. A mere verbal pun is, as a rule, and except in the case of names, as little understood by a Sussex man as by a Scotchman ; but humour in idea, heightened possibly, and in my own case certainly, by the unconscious drawl with which it is frequently given, rarely fails of success.

Many years ago there was a man in " Heffle " (Heathfield) parish, the next parish to our own on the west, who, having a small annuity, lived upon it in idleness. Low as his credit was, he had managed to get considerably into debt, and the visits of his creditors in the hope of getting their money were frequent and pressing. The man was not an early riser, and persons who specially wanted to find him at home would make sure by calling before he was up. One morning a neighbour knocked at the door, and insisted on the man's wife rousing her husband, and compelling him to settle an account. She accordingly went upstairs, woke her husband, and failing, as usual, to get any money, said, rather sharply—

" I wonder, John, you can lie sleeping there when you owe all the money you do."

" Oh, I can sleep very well," he said, " if I do owe money ; but," turning round for another snore, he added, " I sometimes do wonder how they can sleep that I owe money to."

A similar contrast between an anxious mind and an easy one I once heard from a stranger in a train, who was telling me of an interview which, soon after he set up in business for himself, he had with a friend who, having been in business a little more than a year, was already hopelessly insolvent, and had several writs out against him, and yet seemed perfectly calm and unconcerned.

" I said to him," added my companion, " ' I wonder however you manage to take things as easy as you do. Why, I can pay twenty shillings in the pound, and yet often and often I can't sleep for thinking.'

"'Ah,' he said, 'that's just the difference between us. You can't sleep for thinking, and I can't think for sleeping.'"

I do not affirm that a true bill would be found upon the following indictment against a parish in the county of Essex, but I do not think that the parishioners themselves would deny that the indictment had been laid. During a season of great drought, the inhabitants of the parish sank a deep well at the public expense. The well having been dug, the large heap of earth which had come out of it was, by common consent, voted an eyesore which ought to be removed. A parish meeting was accordingly held, to consider how the obnoxious heap should be got rid of. Many suggestions were made as to the best way of dealing with it, but at last it was proposed, and unanimously carried, that they should dig a large hole and bury it! How often the process of digging a fresh hole to bury the earth, which had come out of the last, was repeated I never heard, but I fear that the plan must have put the parish to a good deal of expense before it was successful. This, however, was in Essex, not in Sussex. The South Saxon mind occasionally exercises itself in much sterner fashion. The Rev. A. Eden, the worthy vicar of Ticehurst, the next parish to our own on the north, has for many years employed a gardener of the name of Bones, and the fact has been turned to account in the solution of an interesting scientific inquiry. It has been asked, "What evidence does Ticehurst parish afford of the existence of pre-Adamite man?" To which question there is the obvious and sufficient answer, "The discovery of bones in the garden of Eden." Even in the "sheeres," too (which word "shires" a non-Sussex reader may interpret to mean any part of England generally, outside of Sussex, Surrey, or Kent), men's minds are sometimes put to a test before which the reasoning powers that determined the fate of the heap of earth would, I fear, have quailed. A friend once told me that he had himself, as I certainly understood him, held the following colloquy in one of the Midland counties with the proprietor of a clock, which must have involved its owner in habits of serious calculation—

"Why, Mr. Jones, your clock is not quite right, is it?"

"Well, you see, sir," said Mr. Jones, "nobody don't understand much about that clock but me. When the hands of that clock stand at twelve then it strikes two, and then I knows it's twenty minutes to seven."

What the real time was when Mr. Jones's clock struck half-past five would be a not unreasonable question in a Civil Service Examination paper.

A truly rural story, the point of which was certainly rather broader, but which indicated to me no small sense of that humour which I am claiming as a set-off against our country dulness, I had also from a stranger, an elderly farmer, as I took him to be, a fellow-passenger in a train from Salisbury to Grately. Should my unknown friend ever see my version of his tale, I hope that he will pardon me for spoiling it by my indifferent telling, and that he will accept my thanks for the enjoyment which it afforded me. It ran thus, as nearly as I remember. Two Cockneys, who had come down to stay a few days in the country, near Grately, on the borders of Hampshire and Wiltshire, met in their walk one morning an old man, who, my informant said, was "a droll old chap," and who happened to have a large pumpkin under his arm. The Londoners noticed that the old man was carrying something, though they could not quite make out what it was, and confident in their power as town-dwellers, they thought they would have a little joke at the old countryman's expense. So they opened fire.

"Good morning, master."

"Good marnin', zur."

"What is that you are carrying under your arm, friend ? "

"'Tis a mare's egg, zur."

"Dear me ! " said the Londoners, not liking to own their ignorance ; "it's the finest we ever saw."

"Ah, zur," said the old man, "there's lots of common uns about, but this is a thoroughbred un, zur ; that's what makes un look so vine."

"Will you sell it ? " said the Cockneys.

"Well," said the old man, "I doan't mind partin' wi' un, tho' I doan't s'pose you'll give me the money I want for a thoroughbred mare's egg."

After some bargaining, the men put their hands into their pockets and paid what was asked. The old man then handed over the pumpkin, and as he did so, looked at them very seriously, and said—

"Now, mind, zur, and do 'ee take great care wi' un, for she'll hatch soon ! "

Away went the Londoners with their mare's egg, and as they were crossing a hill just by Grately station, which my informant pointed out, the one who was carrying the prize stumbled over one of the juniper bushes with which the hill is dotted about, and dropped the pumpkin, starting at the same time a hare out of the bush. In their excitement, and thinking, I suppose, that the fall had suddenly hastened the hatching, they shouted wildly to some men at work in a field at the bottom of the hill—

" Hi ! stop our colt ! stop our colt ! "

The story, told as it was in the purest Wiltshire dialect, was truly amusing.

It is, however, a curious illustration of the temptation to give an air of reality and a proportionately increased interest to an anecdote by assigning it to a particular person or locality. When I heard the story in the train, and saw my friend point out the very scene of it on the hill at Grately, I felt that I was receiving it fresh from the very fountain-head. To my surprise, however, I found only the other day that the narrative in almost identical words was a favourite one of the father of one of my own parishioners, a Kentish man born and bred, who had been a resident all his life in his own county. I have since also been assured by a friend in the next parish, that her late husband's father, a Scotchman, living twenty miles beyond the border, used to tell this very same story with the greatest satisfaction. Where, therefore, it took its rise, and how it became known in districts so wide apart as Wiltshire, Kent, and the Lowlands of Scotland, are questions which I, at any rate, am not able to answer.

How far I may have been the victim of a like illusion in other stories I cannot say. I tell them after due inquiry as they were told me, and time and circumstances are no invention of my own. Having thus warned my readers, I disclaim further responsibility. Occasionally, I must confess, I feel somewhat inclined to shelter myself behind a dictum which I have heard attributed to Dr. Johnson. Some one had, unluckily for himself, told the doctor a story with such an air of truthfulness that the doctor had accepted it as true, and on being laughed at for his credulity, he is said to have retorted with Johnsonian force—

" Sir, you take me for a fool because I did not take you for a liar."

A great many years ago, so the tradition is, our village miller was asked by a good solicitor, who was occasionally fond of a joke outside the limits of the profession, how the saying had got about that there was never but one miller who went to heaven.

" Oh, sir ! " replied Mr. Skinner, the miller, " and shall I tell you how it was that he ' bid ' there [i.e. stopped there] when he was there ? "

The good lawyer gave it up.

" Because, sir," said the miller, " they couldn't find never a lawyer there to e-ject him. Good morning, sir."

I am quite aware that an epigram involving the same point with reference to priests, is attributed to Dean Swift, but our miller's humour was none the less original, for I think we may rest assured that he had never heard of Dean Swift.

There is, no doubt, always a danger of telling stories which are already known, even in quoting what one believes to be the most purely local efforts of the rural mind. If, however, I am detected in crediting Sussex or any other county with humour, or supposed humour, not its own, I can only say again, in self-defence, that I most conscientiously refrain from giving, without due warning, as a " recollection," anything which I have ever heard anywhere else than in the county, or which I have the least ground for supposing is not the genuine offspring of native imagination.

Here is another tradition which in my early Sussex days fixed itself in my memory, and which has been stamped as true to Sussex nature by every local audience before which I have produced it. At a meeting of our guardians, a man was applying for more relief. A difficulty, as is often the case, presented itself in the unthriftiness of the wife, and the fact was notified to the applicant in the not uncommon formula—

" We are afraid, Master Smith, that your wife is not a very good manager."

" Oh ! gentlemen," replied Master Smith, " I don't know naun about my wife not being a good manager ; but I do know one thing—I know she could manage a good deal more if she could get it."

I have heard also that, on a suggestion being made at our petty sessions to a man whose character for sobriety was not very high, that it was to be feared that he was a good deal given to drink, the immediate reply was vouchsafed by the unabashed defendant—

" No, gentlemen ; there you be quite wrong ; it's a good deal of drink as is given to me."

His defence being that people had treated him, and that so he was overcome.

I have so constantly been worsted in my word encounters with men whose wits have been unduly sharpened by a little drink, that I have long ago given up speaking to them either in the way of reproof or of exhortation or in any way at all if I can possibly avoid doing so, Before, however, I had learnt wisdom, I one day begged a man, a stranger to me, who was making a terrible noise in our churchyard, to make his noise, if he made it at all, somewhere else than close to the church. On being spoken to, the man drew himself up with all the dignity he could command, and said—

" Who be you ? "

I answered—

" Oh, that is no consequence. I am the curate."

" Curate ! " he said ; " and what if you be ? What be you speaking to me for ? I be a bishop ! "

Just at this moment his mate came up, and said—

" Oh, sir, never mind him, sir—his name's Bishop, that's all.

Such an answer as this unfortunately obliterates in our people's minds all idea of wrong-doing by reason of the drink, and the humour entirely condones the sin.

At times the meaning of our repartees is a little more recondite, and does not lie absolutely on the surface. More than once, at a Club dinner, or some similar entertainment, I have heard, during a pause after the pudding, and before the cloth was drawn, the following conversation :—

" I say, Bill, I think I've lost somethin' sin' I came into this room " ; and Bill, without condescending to guess what the something was, has replied—

" Oh, never you mind ; you'll find it again to-morrow morning without looking for it."

The term, " without looking for it," as applied to the re-discovery of the appetite, has struck me as ingenious.

Even our boys occasionally shine, though it may be unconsciously. A carter-boy on a clay soil, whose life is physically a very trying one, may be excused for being dull and slow ; and the following explanation by a young carter's mate of an accident which happened to one of his horses is, I fear, above the average ;

still I give it as it was told me at the time. We then happened to have in the parish one team of horses so lean and poor that they looked more like skeletons than working animals, and their heads, as in skeletons, seemed large and heavy, and out of proportion to their bodies. The accident was a kick which one of the poor brutes had given another in the stable, and the carter-boy being called upon for his version of the affair, was reported to me as having said—

"Well, you see, somehow he's head fell out of the manger"—how this first step came about he did not pretend to say, but this being assumed, the rest was simple—" and that overbalanced his body, so he's hind leg flew up and het agen t'other horse, and that's jus' how 'twas."

That the poor animal had spirit or strength enough to kick at all, was an idea that the boy could not entertain for a moment, so the theory of the head overbalancing the body was the only explanation he could suggest.

I have heard another young Sussex carter-boy credited with the following piece of bold, if somewhat cynical, advice to his father, whose " mate " he was. In their team of four horses, three, either through temper, or laziness, or poor condition, if there was any more than common difficulty, refused to draw. The wagon was " stood," and the carter naturally began to use his whip to the unwilling horses. His son, after watching for awhile the uselessness of the proceeding, cried out—

" Lash into him, father, as will draw ; what's the good of lashing into them as won't ? "

A younger boy still was once also, I am sure, singularly unconscious of the amusement which his answers to some questions which I happened to ask him in the street of our village afforded me. Not knowing whose boy he was, I said—

" Well, my little man, whose little man are you ? "

He—" Father's."

I—" Quite right ; but where do you live ? "

He—" Along wi' father."

I—" Yes, yes ; but where does your father live ? "

He—" Why, he's our father—he lives along wi' us."

I retired discomfited.

A good many years ago a gentleman, a relation of my own, had not much better success with a boy of Ticehurst parish, who was marking for him during a day's shooting. The boy had been especially stupid, and at last the gentleman, almost in despair, fixed him in a spot where there was a good view, and gave him the simple order—

" Now, when you hear me fire, and shout ' Mark ! ' do you take especial notice where the birds settle."

In due course a shot was fired, and " Mark ! " was called. When the gentleman came up to the boy, he asked him—

" Well, Tom, where did those birds settle ? "

" Down there, sir, under that gurt oak tree."

Not a bird, however, was to be found.

The gentleman returned.

" Tom, you stupid boy, where did those birds settle ? "

" Down there, sir, under the gurt oak tree."

" Why, there isn't a bird there."

" Well, sir, I know that's where they settled, for as soon as I see 'em settle, I thought I'd go down alongside the hedge just to make sure, and soonsever

I popped my head over to see if they was there, hanged if they didn't all get up and fly away! but I be sartin that's where they settled."

The following answer, which I once got from one of our young men to whom I was speaking on the advantage of having a home of his own instead of knocking about in lodgings, is, I am told, not confined to Sussex. I heard it, however, in our street, and I have never heard it anywhere else, so it is Sussex to me. The young man listened patiently to what I had to urge, and then delivered his judgment.

" I don't seem to see the good of giving some woman half my victuals to get t'other half cooked."

The unconventional turn which rustic answers take often puts the questioner sorely at a disadvantage, and sheer unpreparedness leaves the victory with the enemy.

My father used to tell me of an unexpected speech of this kind made to a gentleman whom he knew in his early days, which would certainly have left me at a loss for a reply.

The good man was out driving with his wife, who was noted for her bad temper, and, in a narrow road, met a wagon which they had some difficulty in passing. The lady, apparently thinking that the carter was not making as much haste as he ought to do to get out of the way, began to rate him pretty freely. Just, however, as they drew clear, the man stepped up to the carriage, and, respectfully touching his hat to the gentleman, asked whether he might speak a word. The lady, thinking that he was going to apologize for his slowness, interposed, and said very sharply—

" Yes, say whatever you have got to say."

Whereupon the man, again touching his hat, and looking hard at the gentleman, said very quietly—

" Sir, I do pity'ee from the bottom of my heart, for I've got just such another brute at home myself."

Not long ago I heard also of the experience of a clergyman in the north country, if I remember right, which I should think somewhat crippled the power of rejoinder. As he was riding one day, rather in a hurry, he saw ahead of him a small boy with a barrow, who was gathering road manure, but who had drawn up by the roadside, evidently wishing to speak to him. He accordingly stopped his horse, and had no sooner done so than the boy inquired, in perfect innocence—

" Oi say, mester, have yo seen any muck along th' road ? "

At such a moment dignity is at a discount, and riding on as quickly as possible seems the only resource.

How a former well-known Master of Balliol College, Oxford, fared, when, in an encounter with a turnpike man, riding on was the one particular remedy for shattered dignity which was denied him, the story does not say. The tradition, however, is that the good " master," coming to a turnpike gate in a part of the country where he was not known, found, on putting his hand into his pocket, that he had left all his money at home. The gatekeeper would not let him pass, whereupon the " master," little accustomed to be thwarted by anybody, and much less by a rustic, showed signs of wishing to force his way, expostulating in utter amazement—

" But, my good man, it will be all right ; I am the Master of Balliol."

" Don't care what you're master of, but if you aren't master of twopence you don't go through this gate," was the inexorable but somewhat cruel reply.

I was myself once utterly at a loss for a suitable rejoinder when, finding a boy of about fifteen smoking, I unadvisedly tried the line of banter, by saying—

" Oh, Harry, Harry ! if you don't mind you'll be a man before your time."

And received for my answer—

" Oh, you should see me at my knife and fork ; I just be a trencherman."

I felt that a homily after such a spirited resistance would fall very flat, and I did not pursue the subject.

I have often greatly envied the powerful formula which I have heard attributed to a publican who in former times kept the " Gun " at Netherfield. If any lad whom he thought of too tender years to have begun to smoke called for half an ounce of tobacco, he would ask—

" Who for ? Is it for your father ? "

And if the boy answered, " No ; it's for myself," he would say, " Go along with you, and buy a penn'orth of bull's-eyes ; I've not learnt my hog to smoke yet, and I'm not going to serve you."

I heartily wish that this moral courage was more plentiful in these more polite days.

Were it not for a discrepancy of dates, my young trencherman might have been the very boy whose fame has come down to us in connection with the power of appetite. He had been sent with a message to a Squire's house a few miles from Burwash, and was set down by the cook to the very considerable remains of a round of beef, and told to help himself, while he waited for his answer. The answer found him still occupied ; and the cook, as unwisely as myself, spoke jestingly, and said—

" Well, my little man, are you going to finish it ? "

Her helplessness was as complete as my own when the boy said, very seriously, as he ate on—

" Well, ma'am, I think I could—leesurely."

I do not know that it is wise to be the chronicler of one's own defeats, but possibly my confession may be useful in putting on his guard some good country curate as inexperienced as I once was.

I have not a second time fallen into the trap, which either wittingly or unwittingly was once successfully laid for me by one of my National schoolboys, who, in defiance of a well-known rule, was sucking bull's-eyes during lesson-time. His cheek bulged out so obtrusively, that I could not overlook the breach of discipline. I accordingly opened the window and told him to throw away the illegal bolus. He slowly, but without demur, walked up to the window, and then, in the presence of the whole class, just as I expected him to put his finger into his mouth and take out the cause of offence, gave a terrible gulp, which showed with painful distinctness the destination of the lump as it passed down his throat, and said with a perfectly vacant and unconscious look—

" It's all gone."

I was not ready, and I am afraid that instead of gravely rebuking such indecent behaviour, as I suppose I ought to have done, I heartily joined in the laugh which greeted my discomfiture. The boy's conduct in deferring the upshot of his scheme till such public attention had been called to it, was really as cruel as that of a Winchester boy of generations gone by, of whom my father used to tell me, that being somewhat deaf, he waited till Dr. Gabell had completely finished a long and very serious public reprimand, and then assured him in a most penitent voice—

" I'm very sorry, sir, but I haven't heard one single word you've said."

III

THE humour of the following colloquy, which I once overheard in our village, strikes me as real—

" You be afeerd of hard work, you be," said one of the disputants.

" No I bain't," said the other ; " I'd lie down and go to sleep alongside of it any day. I bain't afeerd of it."

A somewhat more elaborate specimen of the quality of humour which I am claiming as a counteracting set-off against the dulness of our country life, took, some five and twenty or thirty years ago, the form of a practical joke. An old man, Phil Ladds by name, who had a great reputation as a quack doctor, used to travel week by week through these parts. One day a servant-girl came to see him, and said—

" I'm troubled with two bad complaints, Mus. Ladds, and I want you to cure 'em. I've got a lyin' tongue and a bad memory, and I jus' should be glad if you could get rid an 'em for me."

" Ah, well," said the doctor, " I haven't got the right stuff with me for those complaints to-day, but you come again when I'm round this way next week, and I'll set you all right."

In the meantime the doctor made up a couple of pills of asafœtida, or some such nauseous compound, and when the girl in due course presented herself again, he gave them to her, telling her to take one there and then, in the shop, and to chew it well, or else it would not do her the least atom of good. As soon as the girl began to chew she began to spit and splutter, and cried out—

" Oh, Mus. Ladds, this is just beastly stuff you've given me ; I can't swallow it nohows in de wurreld."

" Ah, there," said the doctor, " you've spoke the truth, that's certain, so I've cured your lying tongue ; and I'm sure you won't forget that pill, so I've cured your bad memory. I shan't charge you nothing ; good morning."

Another harmless practical joke, not without its ludicrous side, was perpetrated, in the ruder days of our " Common," upon an old man, a neighbour, who was noted for his powers of talking.

A carter, after racking up his horses one night, had gone out with another man, as the moon was shining, to cut some litter, and while doing so they caught sight of their friend coming towards them. The idea suddenly struck them that they would try and see for once how long the old man would talk if he got a fair chance ; so they drew him into conversation, sat down upon some of the heaps of litter, and there sat talking till it was time for them to think of going home and seeing about breakfast.

The nearest approach to this feat that I have heard of was made by two of our farmers, who are long since dead, but who, within the memory of many, were living about a mile from each other, and who kept walking backwards and forwards along the lane between their respective houses, seeing each other home, and talking, from nine in the evening till three the next morning, when they separated.

Many years ago a somewhat superior " Cockney," who had come down from London for " hopping " at Southover Farm, realized one form of Sussex humour also in a practical shape. He had annoyed a good many of our " home-dwellers " by his ill-disguised contempt for " yokels " and " country bumpkins," and a punishment was accordingly prepared for him.

Three of our natives took occasion one morning, when he was standing near them, to say in rather loud tones that in the evening they were going owl-catching. The bait was swallowed. The Londoner turned round and eagerly asked to be allowed to join them. They agreed, but only on condition that he held the sieve to catch the owls as they fell. This he was perfectly ready to do.

In the course of the day, two of the men, having got a long ladder, put two buckets full of water on a broad beam that went across the top of the barn.

As soon as it was dark they proceeded with their friend to search the barn for owls. The holder of the sieve they very carefully put exactly under the beam with strict orders to stand still while they went up to turn the owls out. The result is more clearly foreseen by the reader than it was by the Cockney. He had not stood long where he was placed before the buckets were emptied, and thoroughly explained to him a " yokel's " idea of " owl-catching " in Southover barn.

This form of humour—dry humour we can hardly call it—seems also to have been known in Kent, inasmuch as one of my parishioners tells me that forty years ago, in the parish of Sandhurst, he was unsuccessfully invited to join in the sport.

A practical joke played upon a police-constable

3

whom I once knew in another part of the country, I may also quote as typical of rural humour.

The young man, a fine upstanding fellow, was satisfactory except on the score of intelligence. The authorities, feeling that this drawback somewhat disqualified him for the service, wished him to resign, but could find no sufficiently distinct cause for obliging him to do so. After a time, however, they applied a test which they considered would be sufficient, if it succeeded, to justify them in requesting him to retire.

The superintendent addressing him one day said—

" Smith, a sawpit has been stolen at Goose Green ; I wish you to go over and try and find out who has got it."

The constable's ready obedience to the order, and his walk of some miles to carry out his investigation settled the question of his continuance in the force.

For anything I know this may have been a standard joke in the service ; still the imagination which invented the test could not have been of the melancholy character which is, I imagine, often attributed to our rustic intellect.

A repartee, which never loses its reward of applause, is recorded as having been made to old Master Barnard, a shoemaker, who formerly lived in our street. A sturdy vagrant was begging at his door one Christmas-time, and Master Barnard, thinking that the man was able-bodied enough to work said, rather indignantly—

" No, I've got nothing to give you ; a strong, able bodied man like you ought to get a trade and work at it, as I'm forced to do."

" I do work at my trade when I can get work," said

The Burwash Ridge, with Church in Distance

the man, " but there's nothing much doing in my trade just now."

" Your trade ! " said old Barnard ; " I wonder what sort of a trade yours is ? "

" I'm a haymaker by trade," said the man, " and my trade's very slack this Christmas-time."

As an illustration of the long life which awaits a bit of real humour in our quiet country districts, I have heard just lately the following story told twice, and by persons so far removed from each other that the tradition of the anecdote is evidently preserved not only in but beyond the parish which gave it birth. About ninety years ago the Vicar of Burwash was one Archdeacon Courtail, whose name was locally pronounced Kirtle. One Sunday afternoon a man, not quite sober, had strayed into the church, and hearing some sentence in the sermon which, in his half-drunken state, he thought was meant for himself, he called out—

" Don't rub too hard, Kirtle."

The utterance was allowed to pass unnoticed, but shortly afterwards the sentence being unfortunately repeated, the unhappy man again called out—

" Don't rub too hard, Kirtle ; I told you not to rub too hard."

This renewed interruption could not be overlooked, and the Archdeacon accordingly stopped, and requested the churchwardens to remove the man from the church. The request was obeyed, and as the irreverent offender was being led through the west door he stammered forth the still remembered sentence—

" Well, I never got into any trouble yet but what I always found friends to help me out."

Another story I have also heard within the last

year or two ; and though it cannot boast the age of
the last, still, as it dates from our bad times between
1825 and 1836, it has been fairly well preserved.

A labouring man, out of work and hungry, went
one morning into the surgery of a neighbouring
parish doctor, sat down, and asked to have one of his
teeth taken out.   The doctor opened the man's mouth
and looked at his teeth, but seeing nothing amiss,
said—

" Which is the tooth, friend ? "

" Oh, e'er a one you like, sir," said the man.   " I've
got nothin' for 'em to do, so I thought I might as well
get rid an 'em."

The good doctor did not charge his patient anything
for looking into his mouth, but gave him a shilling,
and told him to go and get his teeth a job for one day
at all events.

Concerning teeth, not of men, but of dogs, my good
friend the medical man of the next parish to my
own, tells me that some time ago, as he was calling at
a house, the door was opened by a genuine, simple,
somewhat uncouth Sussex maiden, past whom rushed
out two dogs, which began to snarl uncomfortably
near his heels.   Not quite liking their ways, he said
to the girl—

" I hope your dogs don't bite ? "

" I reckon they wouldn't make out much if they
didn't," was the only reply.

It was not all at once that the full meaning of the
answer revealed itself to the doctor's mind, but on
reflection it struck him that dogs that couldn't bite
their food would " make out " badly in feeding, and
he was reassured.

Our native domestics have at times done their share

in unconsciously amusing us. A clever young cook whom I once knew in this part of the county, used frequently to mention among the advantages she had had, the special one of being for a time kitchen-maid under a religious cook. I chanced one day to inquire the point of view from which this fact was regarded as so beneficial, and the answer I found was this, that the cook being religious had a class in a Sunday school, and that in consequence all the Sunday cooking fell to the lot of the kitchen-maid, whose experience was thereby greatly enlarged.

In former years I knew well a Sussex curate of an uncomplaining turn of mind, whose landlady one morning apologized to him for the charcoal-like condition of his toast, on the ground that the servant had " cooked it too rash," that is, had toasted it in such a hurry that she had burnt it to a cinder. The mistress had said to the girl—

" Surely you are never going to take that in to the gentleman ; why, a dog wouldn't eat it," or words to that effect.

" Oh, I lay he will," was the reply, and in the toast had come.

Greater consideration, however, for an employer was, I confess, shown by a young East Sussex cook, who, when on entering upon her new situation she saw the state in which the saucepans had been left by her predecessor, said most feelingly—

" I grieved over them as if they had been my own mothers."

The doctrine that the present is a restless age, and that the members of a household feel that they need frequent change, is one which, in my own experience at least, is, I am thankful to say, by no means borne out by facts. Still we have some restless maidens, no doubt, as a lady who formerly lived in the parish, and who happened to be in want of a parlour-maid, could testify. She told me that, among other applicants for the place was an uncultivated damsel who did not look much more than sixteen or seventeen years of age. She added—

" I naturally remarked, ' You are rather young for such a situation, are you not ? '

" ' Oh,' said the girl, ' I am ever so much older than I look.'

" ' But,' I inquired, ' have you ever had a situation before ? '

" ' Oh yes, lots ! ' was the prompt reply."

The girl was not accepted. Much of the changing of situations, however, among our younger girls is not to be wondered at. They go for their first place to the seaside lodging-houses, where the work is too much for them, and they are obliged to leave.

As regards service in our farmhouses, it seems to be generally admitted that the work required in modern times is nothing when compared with that expected from the servants of former days. The following description of a Sussex farm-servant girl's life fifty or sixty years ago I got from an old parishioner as her own experience, and I have every reason to believe it to be perfectly genuine, and to be a no very exaggerated instance of farmhouse service at the time of which she spoke.

" Massy ! " she said, " the girls nowadays don't know naun about work ! When I was sixteen years old I was had out, like a cow, to the market, and any farmer who wanted a servant come and choosed one.

I went first as nurse-girl, and I got 1s. 3d. a week. Then I went to ' Early ' farm in Wadhurst parish, and there I was to have 1s. 6d. a week—but then I'd more work to do. I'd churning twice a week, and cheesing twice a week, and brewing twice a week, beside washing and baking ; and six cows to milk ' every ' night and morning, and sometimes a dozen pigs to feed. There were four men lived in the house, and I'd all the bilin' to do—the cabbage and the peas and pork for their dinners—besides all the beds to make ; and sometimes I did make 'em in a fashion, that's sartin ! One morning, I mind, I got up at four and worked till twelve at night, and then missus wanted me to pick a couple of ducks.

" ' No, missus,' I says, ' I really can't ; I be quite tired.'

" ' Tired ? ' says she ; ' if I was a young woman like you I should be ashamed of myself ! '

" Ah ! it just was a treat to get an hour or two to one's self of a Sunday ! I was twelve years servant at 1s. 6d. a week, and then I got married ; and when my husband died I went to service again, and for all I'd bin a married 'ooman, I only got 1s. 6d.! After a while I got 2s. a week, and then a man, who'd bin a soldier, wanted somebody as could work to kip house for him, and he gave me 2s. 6d. a week. Massy ! the gals nowadays don't know naun about work."

One must rejoice that such a life as this is no longer the lot of our young women—even though the balance may have gone down too far on the other side.

It is hard to believe that the young life of this good woman and her contemporaries is separated by only one generation from that of a class of elder Sunday school girls of somewhat similar social rank—viz. domestic servants to be—whom a relation of my own was entertaining two or three years ago at tea. At seven, or half-past seven, the hostess—it being her own dinner-hour—sent down a message to her guests, who had been enjoying themselves since an early hour in the afternoon, that they could now go home. To this message the reply was promptly returned—

"Please, miss, when we're asked out to a party we don't go home till nine ! "

There would not be much use, I fear, in asking any one of those young women to wash, and bake, and brew, and milk cows, and feed pigs, and to do work in general from morning to night.

One of my former parishioners, who has now long been settled in London, but who in his young days knew thoroughly well the lot of a Sussex carter-boy, tells me that every now and then an employer in the olden time was noted for keeping a poor table for the men and boys in the house, as well as for expecting a good deal of work from them ; and he gives me a rhyme current in his youth concerning a farm just beyond the borders of our parish, which does not show the attractive side, at any rate, of a labourer's life fifty years ago—

" Pork and cabbage all the year,
  Mouldy bread and sour beer,
    Rusty bacon, stinking cheese,
    A chaff bed full of fleas,—
  Who do you think would live here ? "

The following anecdote, vouchsafed to me by a district visitor in London as true of two young semp-stresses within her own knowledge, has, I own, nothing to do with either Sussex or servant-girls, but it has to do with the class from which our servants come, and with the development of modern ideas in that class, and so I give it a place. The two girls invested their hard-earned savings of a twelvemonth in a day's drive in a brougham in the parks and elsewhere, a clause being specially inserted in the agreement with the livery-stable keeper that the footman should touch his hat and say, " My lady ! "

An old man to whom I was speaking not long since would scarcely have been able in his young days to have enjoyed himself on his year's savings in like manner, even if the idea had entered his mind, for he tells me that in 1815, being fifteen years old, he lived for twelve months as farm-servant in the house with a farmer about a mile from the village, at no wages, the parish finding him clothes, and that at the end of the year, when he left, his master gave him a shilling in token of complete satisfaction with his conduct ! And yet from this beginning the old man has saved enough to maintain himself in his old age without being beholden to the parish. I only hope that the modern enlargement of our ideas will not displace the dogged perseverance and pertinacity of purpose which many of our old people have shown in their striving for independence. I have often thought that there was a shrewdness which foretold more than ordinary success in life in the preparation for the struggle which one of our ancients made in the early part of this century, by investing the first guinea he ever saved in having the small-pox by inoculation. It was a singular turn for a young man's ideas to take, but the result justified the outlay—insomuch, at least, as that he escaped all further attacks of small-pox, and lived to a vigorous old age of eighty-two.

A remarkable instance of mental force, coupled with physical weakness, I met with in an old man, a contemporary and neighbour of our last-mentioned friend. At the age of eighty he was laid down and confined to his bed by a paralytic seizure, and at that age, and under those unpromising conditions, taught himself to read. That he knew his letters I think not improbable, but I forgot to make inquiry on this point. To be sure of the fact that he could read, I asked him one day to read me a few verses in the New Testament, and I well remember his saying, as he stopped to take a good look at some longer word than usual, such as " synagogue "—

" Three months ago, sir, I wasn't man enough to say that word—no, nor yet ' Jeruzalem ' nother ! "

The late Bishop Milman, Bishop of Calcutta, we are told, learnt Persian, Bengali, and Hindustani after he was fifty years old, and the latter well enough to be able to give fluently a lecture of an hour and a half to an audience of educated natives ; but I am inclined to think that our old paralysed, bed-ridden limeburner, teaching himself to read " synagogue " and " Jerusalem " after he was eighty, is not altogether unworthy of mention in connection with even the bishop's marvellous power.

The mention of a bishop suggests one piece of grim humour connected with our parish, which, though not itself the produce of our own soil, comes down to us from antiquity. The son of one of the lords of the manor became Bishop of Lincoln, and Dr. Wordsworth, the present occupant of that see, in his charge delivered in the year 1873, records a visitation held by Bishop Burgwash in the year 1334. The bishop, though he was twice Lord Treasurer, and held other high offices, was apparently of little worth, for Fuller the Antiquary writes of him, that when we have allowed that he was of noble birth, we have said all that is to be said in his commendation, he being otherwise neither good for Church nor State, sovereign nor subjects; covetous, rebellious, ambitious, injurious. Among the bishop's many failings was an undue fondness for sport, and in order to gratify his taste more freely, he made during his episcopacy a park, by ejecting his poorer tenants from their holdings, and enclosing the land with palings. It is, however, reported that after his death his well-earned punishment came upon him; and we read that his ghost appeared to a certain person, who had been one of his esquires, in the garb of a keeper—short green coat, with his bow, quiver, and bugle-horn—and thus addressed him:

"Thou knowest how I have offended God and injured the poor by enclosing this park. For this reason I am called upon to do penance as keeper thereof until such time as it is laid open again. Go therefore to my brethren the canons of Lincoln, and beseech them in my name to restore to the poor people what I have so unrighteously taken from them."

It is not said who was the author of the pious fraud, but his grim humour was successful. Brother William Bachelor was commissioned by the canons to attend to the matter; the palings were destroyed, the ditches filled up, and the poor tenants, we trust, came to their land again.

A long interval was apparently necessary to produce any further effort of humour worthy of being treasured in history in connection with our parish. Some time, however, before the year 1662, one

Thomas Goldham was our Vicar, and in Palmer's "Nonconformist Memorial" we have the following story told of him. Soon after his entrance on the ministry he was disturbed by a Quaker, who, entering his church, and walking towards the pulpit as a ghost, said to him—

" I am sent with a message from God to thee."

Mr. Goldham then asked him : " Dost thou know my name ? "

" Nay," said the Quaker, " I know it not."

Mr. Goldham replied : " If God had sent thee to me He could have told thee my name," and endeavoured to convince him that if he did not know his name he might be mistaken as to the person he was sent to. At this the man was confounded, and the people were satisfied without any dispute. Some years ago there was a question when or where Mr. Goldham was buried, and my inquiries were set at rest by a curious piece of evidence. An old man told me that he knew it was in 1691 ; and when I asked how he was able to be so certain, he told me that when he was a boy he used to play in the churchyard where the tombstone of a Mr. Thomas Goldham was broken and lying about, and he remembered the date because it was the same whether it was the right way up or upside down. I at once went to the register and found directly among the burials the entry of Thomas Goldham, December 31, 1691. 1881 being passed, we must wait till 1961 for a similar proof of a date.

IV

SHORTLY before the new Poor Law came into operation, and when our times were almost at their worst, we had a labour farm, called the "Bough Farm," on which were employed, at the expense of the parish, fifty or sixty persons for whom employment could not be found elsewhere. A labourer on the farm happening one day to pick up a dead robin, was struck with the sudden humour of giving the robin a public funeral, and such was the powerlessness of authority at the time, that two days were actually wasted by all the hands on the farm in carrying out this curious freak.

The social state of our parish at that time it is now very difficult to realize. I have before me the copy of an official return of our churchwardens and overseers for the year 1825, by which it appears that out of a population which in 1821 had been estimated at between 1600 and 1700, "the number of persons who had been relieved permanently" during the year was 782, and "the number of persons who had received casual relief during the year was 75," making a total of 857 paupers, out of 1700 inhabitants. The "total disbursement for actual relief to the poor" during the year amounted to £3078 12s. 11d., and the total parochial expenditure for the same time to £4299 5s. 0¼d. I have not the valuation of the parish for the assessment of the poor-rate for 1825 by me ; but in 1818 the whole rental of the parish, the area of which is 7277 acres, was computed for poor-rate purposes at £3912 10s., and the poor-rate itself for that year was 26s. in the pound on the assessment, though it must not be left out of sight that the assessment was confessedly little more than half the value ; still, 13s. in the pound on the true value was a crushing burden.

The official return for the year ending March 25, 1878, gives our total amount of poor-law expenditure, including county rates and the like, as £1125 10s. 7d. Our assessment is now £10,450, and our population 2232, so that times are indeed changed for the better in this respect.

A parochial broad-sheet published in the agricultural interest in the year 1830, after a series of calculations, brings out the annual loss on farming operations within the parish as £15,488 17s. 6d. !—a statement, indeed, amply justifying the pathetic paragraph which follows : " Which annual loss clearly accounts for the farmers having become so reduced that they are obliged to give up their occupations ; and as others succeed, they also share the same fate, and are obliged to give place to others, and at length the farmers generally are on the brink of ruin. This statement is not peculiar to the parish of Burwash, but will apply to the agricultural parishes generally in this part of the county." As the paper is headed " Yearly Average of Payments and Receipts on Land for Eight Years ending Michaelmas, 1830," and as it sets the total capital invested in agriculture in the parish at £49,000, the average annual loss of £15,488 17s. 6d. during the preceding eight years must no doubt have been serious.

The mathematical powers of our East Sussex folk have never, I imagine, been great ; a weakness which a good old schoolmaster of a past generation, in a neighbouring parish, once turned to account in avenging himself on some agricultural friends who had invited him to dinner, apparently with the design of making him drunk. Their unkind hospitality was but too successful, and the good " dominie " unwittingly fell into the snare. At last, however, finding himself failing, he said, with a sense of conscious superiority even in the moment of his supreme weakness, " Well, gentlemen, if I am drunk, I can ask you a question which you cannot answer. What is two-thirds of three-fourths of a shilling ? " and having said this, he collapsed.

When meetings were being held in this district to promote the Tunbridge Wells and Hastings Railway, one considerable argument employed was the facility which the new line would offer to farmers of getting their produce to market. At a meeting in our own parish a question was put to one of our principal parochial agriculturists, as to how much of our home-grown wheat went out of the parish ? To which inquiry he replied, that he should think, perhaps about three-thirds. Whether the answer attracted any particular attention or not I do not know ; but the audience probably was not critical. It was one of our less highly educated parishioners who always used to plant her potatoes in crooked rows, on the ingenious theory that by doing so she made more of the ground than by planting the rows straight.

Occasionally our calculations, if not mathematical, are, in intention at least, worthy of a district north of the Tweed. A poor woman in our Union having been ordered to take " old " port wine as a tonic, and finding it expensive, was told by the shopkeeper that she could have a newer wine threepence a bottle cheaper. She accordingly bought a bottle a fortnight in advance, calculating that at the end of the time she would have saved threepence, and by having kept the wine so long would still be able to drink " old " port. A more genuine saving than this was effected not long ago by some of my parishioners, who, bringing home from a neighbouring town a vehicle for which a higher toll was demanded than they thought reasonable, took out the horse, paid a three-halfpenny toll for it, and then themselves drew the carriage through for nothing. Had I been the toll-keeper, I should have felt inclined to try the question under the clause " drawn by horse, mule, ox, ass, or any other animal " ; but the point, I believe, was not raised, turnpike philosophy probably not daring to call men " animals."

Among the humours of our village involving calculation, is one touching the five lime trees in our churchyard, which are planted at slightly irregular intervals. I have been told that a quaint old man, whom I knew well, standing with other loungers near the inn at the corner of the churchyard, one day started the question which two of the five trees were planted farthest apart from one another ? After much discussion and mental calculation of distance, resulting in various opinions, he gave his judgment in favour of the two end ones, a conclusion which summarily but satisfactorily disposed of all the guesses, more or less accurate, which had been made as to the distance between other pairs of trees in the row.

Our logic, however, is by no means always so indisputable as this. In a village some miles from ours, an outbreak of typhoid fever, a few years ago, was at last charged upon a milk-seller, whose well was discovered to be foul, and was speedily closed. The good man indignantly repudiated the imputation on his well, and his defence was to his mind ample.

" Why," he said, " I've just had a letter from my sister in Liverpool, and she says that they've had ' titus fever ' down there " ; and he added triumphantly, " now I know they've had naun to do wi' my well down there, that's sartin ! "

If anybody would wish to try the power of pure reason, let him undertake to prove to this good Sussex man the fallacy of his defence.

An old parishioner, in her eighty-sixth year, with whom I was talking the other day about former times, says that she has understood that many people pretend that they would like to live their lives over again. For her part she owns that she certainly should not like to do so, or to face a second time her experience of the past, with flour for a while, before the end of the old war, at 3s. 4d. a gallon, instead of 1s., its common price now ; with salt at 3s. a gallon, instead of 3½d., and with many other things proportionately dear ; the distress, had it not been for the then abundant supply of potatoes, would have been terrible. As it was, the struggle for life was indeed a hard one, and the common formula of our old people in speaking about those days is, that they " cannot begin to tell anybody how they lived "—or else, " Why, there, sir, it wasn't a livin', it was only a bein'." This good woman, whose memory is perfectly clear, gives a most graphic description of the " mobbing " which brought the old poor-law days to a crisis

4

in our parish as well as in others. Years ago I had an account of it from the lips of the man who, one Sunday afternoon, with the words, " Well, mate, what be you gooin' to do—be you gooin' to starve ? " actually collected the first half-dozen of his fellows who began the outbreak, and my informant confirms his statement. Her own husband was seized while at breakfast and compelled to join the mob, which, having been persuaded on its first visit to the village on the Sunday afternoon to disperse, returned in very greatly increased force on Monday morning, and having surrounded one of the principal farmers with a ring of excited labourers, kept him, as it were, prisoner till he gave a promise that he would not use his thresh-ing-machine any more. While some were thus engaged others seized an obnoxious master of the parochial workhouse, and having carried him down to the river which divides our parish from Ticehurst, had given him the alternative of being then and there thrown bodily in, or of promising, on being deposited well over the boundary on the other side the bridge, that he would never show himself in the parish again. If not humorous, the scene is reported to me as having been sufficiently ludicrous.

One of our sources of humour is now nearly dried up. The humanity of modern poor-laws, not unwisely, I hope, removes to public asylums most of the half-witted imbeciles who in former days, being kept at home, used to furnish unfailing sport for the thought-less " lads of the village." Some, however, of the mental efforts of these poor half-wits have obtained an immortality denied to those of their more intelligent brethren.

I well remember one poor fellow, whose only name,

so far as I ever knew, was " Mike." He was credited with several bits of shrewdness or simplicity which are not yet forgotten. He was trying one day to sell as matches at one of our farmhouses some bits of wood, the manufacture of which certainly had not cost him much. The farmer's wife, on looking at them, said—

" Why, Mike, what's the good of bringing these things here ?—they've got no brimstone on them."

" Indeed, ma'am," said Mike, " brimstone do make 'em smell so bad."

The old test of the half-sovereign and half-crown was once applied to him with the full expectation that by reason of the size Mike would prefer the half-crown ; but he was equal to the occasion, and at once picked up the half-sovereign with the remark—

" No, no, Mike won't be covetous. Mike'll be content with the little one."

The last I heard of poor Mike, a good many years ago, was that some one had bribed him to draw his mother, who had lived near the edge of the parish, and who had just died, a little distance over the parish border, so that being found dead in the next parish, the next parish might be obliged to bury her.

This poor Mike Ambleton, or Hambledon, or Hamilton, as I have since learned that he was variously called, seems to have been a wonderfully well-known character in East Sussex, and recollections of him reach me from many quarters. His mother was a native of Sandhurst parish, in Kent, and married in a fit of retaliation for being thwarted by her parents in a match on which she had set her heart. Her husband led her a wandering life, and " Mike " was their only child. One correspondent tells me that he saw the poor " half-wit " go into a barber's shop, in Hastings, one Sunday morning to be shaved, but provided with only one penny instead of two. The barber, however, was quite prepared to meet his customer's limited means, and telling Mike to sit down, speedily shaved the whiskers and beard off one side of his face, leaving the other till the necessary fee was forthcoming.

I am told that once the poor fellow having by some misdemeanour come within the clutches of the law, the magistrates were obliged to commit him to prison for a fortnight, whereupon Mike exclaimed in a pitiful tone of resignation—

" Well, gentlemen, I'll goo—I'll goo ; but I'm sure I shan't like it ! "

Another of our weaker-minded but harmless fellow-creatures was just able to help to dig a grave, and on the occasion of the burial of a man who had been one of his constant tormentors, he had sense enough to jump in upon the earth when the grave was being filled up, and as he stamped down the soil to keep on saying—

" Got ye now, got ye now ! "

I often wonder whether these poor creatures exercise their imperfect intelligence to a like degree in the asylums in which they are gathered. If they do, the note-book of the physician of an asylum for " imbeciles " might be a very treasure-house of unconscious humour. In the earlier part of the century our own village doctor was able, though not by the aid of any of our imbeciles, to contribute one item to our stock of parochial stories, which are useful when ideas run short, and conversation flags. He was scientifically in sufficient advance of his neighbours to keep a rain-gauge, which it was well known he inspected regularly every morning. One night two of his carter-boys—

for he was an amateur farmer as well as a doctor—came to him and said—

" Please, sir, can we go to Mäavul [Mayfield] fair to-morrow ? "

" No, my lads, I don't think I can spare you," said the doctor ; " the fourteen-acre field wants sowing, and we must get at it, if it doesn't rain so hard in the night that we can't get on to the land ; but you come again in the morning."

In the morning the boys duly presented themselves.

" Has it rained in the night ? " asked the doctor.

" Oh yes, sir," said the boys, " very heavy."

The doctor at once went to test their statement by the gauge, and speedily returning, said—

" You young rascals, if it had rained all night three times as hard as it rained at the Flood, it wouldn't have rained into that gauge half of what you've put there."

Knowing very little about the measurement of rain-fall, but knowing that their master judged how much rain had fallen by looking into the gauge, they had in the early morning filled it nearly to the brim. Whether they sowed the fourteen-acre field or not, they probably did not go to Mayfield fair.

Even where stories have no claim to humour, our ancients who have good memories, and who can talk of old times, generally get a hearing for their tales, and though their powers of attraction are lessened no doubt by the growing competition of books and news-papers, " Old Master So-and-so says he remembers " is an introduction which, as a rule, secures respect. These unwritten " Tales of my Grandfather " do duty in our quiet life for the novels and sensational literature which seem to have become an almost necessary complement to those conditions of life which look upon ours as dull and monotonous ; and I very much question whether we do not from time to time find as much to interest us in our *vivâ voce* chronicles as our town brethren do in their books from " Mudie."

And here I may say in passing, lest dwellers in London who are supplied by " Mudie " may think that we in Sussex care little about books, that the Book Club in our own parish has existed for seventy-five years without interruption, the first book that was ordered having been " Cœlebs in Search of a Wife," the orderer being a Mrs. Hussey, in or about the year 1809. As a mere matter of curiosity, I should be glad to know whether many country parishes can produce a longer literary pedigree than this.

On the high ground of Brightling parish, about two and a half miles south of our village, stands an obelisk, called " Brightling Needle," built as a landmark by old Mr. John Fuller, formerly M.P. for the county. It occupies, I believe, the spot on which, in the old war-time, was a beacon always ready to be lighted the moment the long-expected landing of the French in Pevensey Bay should begin to take place.

Some years ago, I was talking to an old man, who in his youth had been one of our bolder spirits. He soon became very earnest in his manner, and in these peaceful days it gave a curious zest to my conversation to feel that I was speaking to a man who had seen people's household goods actually packed on wagons ready to be driven inland. He told me that he was one of the " Sussex Guides " ; and when I asked him what the Sussex Guides had to do, he said, with the ring of well-remembered instructions—

" It was our duty, sir, as soon as we heard of the landing of the French, to repair to the ' George Inn,' at Battle, and thence to guide the army the nearest way to the enemy."

There was a straightforward, business-like sound about such instructions which seemed very real.

When the excitement produced by the strong language of the French colonels asking to be led against " perfidious Albion " was at its height some years since, I was talking to a man of a younger generation, and I asked him, as I looked up at Brightling Hill, what he thought would happen if a signal was given now from " The Needle " that the French were landing ?

" Well, sir," he said, " I think there'd be a good many folks wanting tickets at Etchingham by the next train to London."

No doubt he was right ; but I own that I would gladly have heard some reference made to defence as well as to escape, and I could not help comparing this utterance with the instructions to the " Sussex Guides."

It was curious also in many ways to feel, while talking to this old man, what changes had taken place among us even in one lifetime, and I could well share the feeling of another parishioner who said to me one day—

" Sure-lye there can never be as many changes in the next fifty years as there have been in the last ! "

If any present inhabitant of our parish wishes to realize in some degree the difficulty of transport in Zululand, Ashanti, or any other country without roads, it may help him to be told that a person living in 1871 remembered well that when as a boy he used to carry out meat on horseback, a man was sent with him part of the way, even in the month of May, to take the basket off the horse in some of the worst places, and to put it on again when the horse was safely through, these bad places having been where our soundest road now is. He also remembered six horses being used on the same road to bring up a two-wheeled cart from the mill, the mud coming up to the bottom of the cart. No wonder that travelling on wheels was more rare than it is now, and that he could well remember also farmers' wives in the parish riding on horseback on pillions behind their husbands.

In confirmation of this statement as to the badness of our roads, a resident in Kent, the grandson of one of our former parishioners, sends me the following startling account of the dangers of Sussex travel in bygone days, which was current when he was a boy.

A man walking along the road between Burwash and Ticehurst was surprised to see a hat in the middle of the track. As he passed he gave it a kick, and to his amazement was greeted as he did so with a faint " Holloa ! " He immediately stopped, and under the hat, to his still greater astonishment, he found a man's head. He asked at once what was the matter, and the reply was—

" I am on horseback, and my horse has sunk in the mud ; for mercy's sake help me out ! I am sinking deeper every minute."

Men were collected, and the horse and his rider were dug out. The horse, to the intense surprise of all present, came up with his mouth full of hay, which on further search was found to have been taken from a load that had sunk with a wagon and four horses before the man got there.

As I have not a copy of Baron Munchausen's travels

by me, I cannot say whether the baron ever walked from Burwash to Ticehurst, and so can only give the history as I get it from Kent.

Even at a much later date, when the squire of the neighbouring parish used these same roads at night, his cavalcade consisted of four horses in his carriage, a man riding one of the leaders, a coachman and footman on the box, and a Sussex moon—that is, a man on horseback, with a lantern strapped to his back—leading the way. I have myself been taken in a broad-wheeled wagon to a wedding-breakfast in my own parish, the latter part of the journey to the farmhouse being impracticable for any ordinary carriage ; and within the last three or four years a wagon with a load of bricks for the repair of a farmhouse within sight of the Rectory had to be brought down to its destination with all its four wheels " skidded." These difficulties happen now, of course, only in private lanes ; but these lanes even still are little worse than some of the worst parts of our main high-roads within the memory of man. An eye-witness has told me of lime-wagons " stood " on the high-road from Lewes, and extricated only by faggots placed under the wheels.

The same old man has interested me also in another direction, viz. by enabling me to trace, probably to its extinction as a term in spoken use among us, a word, the last literary use of which Dr. Johnson fixes in 1580. I question whether there is now in the parish anyone who knows practically the meaning of the word " lither." I had heard of its being used, and I questioned my old friend as to its meaning. The word was quite familiar to him in the sense of " idle, lazy." I immediately went to Johnson's Dictionary, where I found it explained in exactly the same meaning.

It is, I own, exceedingly interesting to me to have been in at the death, as it were, in a cottage in our own woods of a word which, having been discarded from books three hundred years ago, had lingered on in common use among our Saxon-speaking folk till my own day. I well know the dangers which beset amateur philologists, and therefore I only mention in connection with the word " lither " the suggestion which I have heard hazarded, that " Lither-pool " is nearer the truth than " Liver-pool," which latter word has necessitated the creation of the " liver," a bird unknown, I am told, to ornithologists. There certainly is a " Lither-land " not far from Liverpool; but then, again, there is a " Lither-mere " not far from Bury St. Edmunds, so I leave the matter; and be it as it may, I have chronicled probably the actual disappearance of " lither " as a spoken word in our parish, after an existence among us of perhaps nearly fourteen hundred years.

A Derbyshire correspondent sends me the following proverb as still common in his county: " As idle as Lithermas dog, which laid himself down to bark."

As a rule, our people are hardly scientific in their attempts at derivation. The name of our parish, which was spelt in the 33rd of Henry III " Bor-wese," and which has, besides Burwash, many other variations of its spelling, I once heard accounted for as follows, by one of my own parishioners, who spoke most seriously—

" When the Romans landed in Pevensey Bay, they had with them a dog, called ' Bur,' and after a while the dog got so bemired with the Sussex clay, that he couldn't travel any further, so they washed him, and the place where they washed him was called ' Burwash.' "

Mr. Rudyard Kipling's House, "Bateman's," Burwash, as restored

The cumulatively hypothetical nature of this derivation greatly pleased me. One of our farmhouses, a fine old Elizabethan mansion, bearing date 1634, is called " Bateman's," and this name I have had explained to me by the tradition that when it was built men's wages were a penny a day, and that the builder wanted to bate something off that, so the house was called " Bateman's " !

A somewhat more tragic derivation is given of the name of another of our farms, which is called " The Bough," from the traditional belief, as I have been told, that a man having been taken prisoner there for murder, pulled a bough out of the hedge and stuck it into the ground, saying that if he was innocent the bough would grow, and that if he was guilty it would die. " Shoyswell " Farm, which is on the borders of our parish, and which gives its name to a hundred of the county, has horseshoes for its sign, as if the name were " Shoeswell " ; but an ingenious parishioner once asked me whether " Shoyswell " might not possibly be a Sussex corruption of the name of some Norman follower of the Conqueror, such as " Choiseuil," a corruption of sound not unlike one which I have had suggested to me as a very simple substitute for the elaborate theories ever and anon invented to explain the " cold harbours " which abound in our county as well as in others. The transition from " col d'arbre " to " cold harbour " is a fairly obvious one, though the suggestion has, of course, to be tested by fact ; and if the situation of " cold harbour " does not, in a reasonable number of instances, satisfy the theory of " col d'arbre," the theory itself is only one of the many which are more ingenious than true.

The dangers of erroneous philology were exemplified

to me in a singular manner a short time since, by one of our own young men. I had occasion to complain of a noise in the belfry, and he had been reported to me as one of the intruders who had shared in the disturbance. I told him that he really must not go up into the belfry again without leave.

" Why not ? " he said. " Haven't I as good a right there as anybody else ? It's ' bell-free,' isn't it ? and it's free to anybody to go up who likes ? "

I could only assure him that, however correct his view of the meaning of the word might be, I was afraid that the law was against him, and that the power of the keys in this instance belonged to the incumbent. For myself, I have been tempted to speculate when I have heard our " road-man " talking about filling in the " wheel trades " after a wet time, whether the term " trade winds " has not really more to do with the steady " track " in which they blow than with trade in any sense of commerce, but the ill success of my " belfry " friend warns me to desist.

V

AMONG the rapidly perishing personal recollections of our old people are those connected with smuggling. I do not think that we have now any parishioners living who actually took part in the smuggling business—for business it really was —but I have heard much from old parishioners who knew all about it, if they did not personally run its risk. A woman has told me that, as a child, she used to say her prayers at night, and then be regularly put to bed with a strict injunction, " Now, mind, if the ' gentlemen ' come along, don't you look out o' window." Peeping at the smugglers was a heinous offence, and was often visited with severe punishment, as it was supposed to give means of identification and detection.

I was once asking an old man in a very wild part of the parish whether the smugglers ever used to store their goods in that district. " I believe you," he said. " Why, this cottage where we be now has many a time been as full of tubs from top to bottom as ever it could hold." He then went on to tell me that his grandfather had had fourteen children, and that he had brought them all up to the smuggling. I asked whether they did not get into trouble. " No," he said, " they were pretty lucky. Uncle Tom he got three months twice in Maidstone Gaol, and then he gave it up, but none of the rest came to no harm." He explained to me the whole arrangements for running cargoes, hiding them up, and getting them into the country. He spoke with perfect openness, and evidently with thorough knowledge. For his own part, I am inclined to think that he somewhat despised our degenerate times, for he assured me that nowadays the liquors were not nearly so good as they used to be ; and I well remember that he added the curious reason, that we did not half know how to adulterate them like the foreigners did. It is nevertheless a great comfort to be able now to go into cottages without the thought that possibly " tubholes " are concealed under our feet, and to be able to look at the floor without suspecting that, by the application of a sucker, a well-fitted brick would come up and reveal a world of spirits to our astonished eyes. The terror inspired by the smugglers was very great, and our excise officer felt it prudent at times to shut his eyes and ears, and to be content with the anker of brandy which lay at his door in the morning, as the reward of his non-interference.

How it was that in the midst of all this lawlessness a learned scholar and poet, Mr. Hurdis, who was curate of the parish, and afterwards Professor of Poetry at Oxford, could write to a friend at the University, " Dear Sir,—Having been expelled by calamity from my little paradise of Burwash, the world is all before me," I cannot tell. By his poem of " The Village Curate," which in its day was very popular, his chief delight seems to have been in physical rather than in human nature ; and as far as wood and hill and dale could give contentment, he had it here, no doubt, in a high degree. An old labouring man, who died at the age of eighty-two or eighty-three, many years ago told me that when he was young he used to go with his mother to work at Mr. Hurdis's, but the poet had left no impression on him, and the learned curate did not differ in his eyes from other curates. Learning, indeed, and science have not hitherto been fully appreciated in our wilds, and though the late Sir John Herschel lived only about seven miles from us, almost within range of an eighty-ton gun, very few of our folk had ever heard of him, and with the few to whom his name was known the wonder was " how he ever made a living by star-gazing ! "

I question, too, whether another notable man who belongs to us has ever had his due share of honour in his own parish. Thomas May, who was born at " The Franchise," in Burwash, accomplished a literary feat which is, I imagine, unique. He boldly wrote a supplement to Lucan's " Pharsalia," and this supplement has so much in common with the original that foreign critics have published it in good editions of Lucan ; and both Dr. Johnson and Mr. Hallam speak of it in terms of high praise. In his after life Thomas May was appointed Secretary to the Parliament, and was by the Parliament commissioned to write the ' History of the Long Parliament," a work of which Mr. Hallam also says, " May's ' History of the Parliament ' is a good model of genuine English : he is plain, terse, and vigorous, never slovenly, though with few remarkable passages, and is in style as well as in substance a kind of contrast to Clarendon."

Alas ! for the reputation of either prose or poetry. Neither May nor Hurdis has left even his name in the parish, and though I once learned a couple of lines of verses from the old man who as a boy went to Mr. Hurdis's, I can hardly suppose that they derived their inspiration from the author of " The Village Curate."

They were part of a song which the old man told me used to be sung in our hop-gardens, and which set forth the marvellous power of hops in drawing to the " bins," at hopping-time, old and young, sick and well, who can possibly stir out-of-doors. He knew only the two first lines, which ran as follows—

" Old Mother Nincompoop had nigh twelve months been dead—
  She heard the hops were pretty good, and just popped out her head."

From this beginning it is possibly as well that his memory at this point failed him. The attractive power of the hop-garden still remains, and, during hopping, times go hard with any invalid who is obliged to stay at home. Last year I heard of a helpless old man who described his daily dinner and the way in which he got it during hopping by the expressive words, " Well, sir, it isn't nothing and it ain't nohow."

As a reward for doing his duty by visiting and mixing in various ways with his parishioners, a clergyman every now and then picks up a bit of wisdom which is a very nugget amid a good deal of less interesting talk. Indeed, I confess that for myself I have often felt the relationship of instructor and instructed curiously inverted in my intercourse with unlearned men and women, the whole cost of whose school education never equalled that of my Latin dictionary, but whose moral rules of thumb and sententious utterances are oftentimes very striking. I do not think that I am far wrong in claiming a high degree of moral instinct for a piece of advice which a poor man told me he had had from his father just before he died. I had come up with the man on the high-road, and after talking awhile about things in general, he began to speak about himself and said—

" Ah, sir, it would have been a good thing for me if I had minded the last words that ever my father said to me. He called me to him and said, ' Now, mind, George,' he said, ' that you always keep better company than you be yourself.' "

My heart sank within me when I thought of all the homilies that I had written and spoken on the subject of companionship ; and how pointless they must have seemed in comparison with this simple sentence of a man who could probably neither read nor write.

The moral question which I now submit to my readers as it was submitted to me, has, I own, no other connection whatever with the previous sentence than a local one. It happened to be propounded to me many years before on just the same spot of road, and so I associate the two conversations. I had overtaken a parishioner who I did not see at the moment was slightly the worse for drink. As I was passing I tendered the usual " Good day," and on the strength of this opening he proceeded to say—

" I've been wanting to see you, sir, for ever so long, and I want you to tell me how 'tis that whenever I get a little drop too much to drink I always feel more religious than I do at any other time."

I will not deny that I was somewhat taken aback by the question ; I certainly had never met with it in my books. What little I knew scientifically about " cases of conscience " did not seem to me to touch the point, and I am afraid that my replies for a minute or two were not of the most lucid order. By degrees, however, I discovered that what the poor man was aiming at was the obtaining my certificate that inasmuch as the drop

5

too much made him feel more religious than common, the drop too much was—well, I hardly think that he expected me to say praiseworthy but, at any rate— very excusable. The feeling religious I took to mean the resolution from time to time not to disgrace himself again. He explained to me that his " transgressions " arose, not out of any love of drink, but from his being a good-natured man, and from his inability to say " No," when friends offered to treat him. All I could do at the moment was to say that he ought to be very thankful that he still had his conscience left to move him to make good resolutions, and that he ought to look upon it as a sign of God's mercy, which might be with- drawn altogether if he went on neglecting it. The certificate of harmlessness in the drink by reason of the good resolutions I could not give. I am thankful to say that my friend, who has been dead some years, had long before his death thoroughly overcome, as far as I knew, any tendency to excess.

One more association with that particular spot I chronicle here because I cannot classify it with any other " recollections," seeing that it is in my experience unique. Close by stood a cottage, since pulled down, tenanted then by a good old body, whose quaint sayings were many. One of them I noted at the time. She was speaking of the sad appearance of a neighbour, and said—

" I don't think I should look as bad as she do ; no, not if I was in my coffin."

Seeing me smile, she added most seriously—

" But you must know, sir, that our family is always noted for carryin' a high colour when we be corpses."

" A beautiful corpse " is a phrase which we, like Sairey Gamp, apply to persons whose appearance after death is placid and peaceful. I was told of a poor woman only the other day, " She was a great sufferer, but she was a beautiful corpse " ; but the " high colour " was an element of posthumous family beauty which I had never heard claimed before.

I do not know that there is anything above the rank of commonplace in a rhyme which was a great favourite of the old man whom I have already mentioned in connection with the word " lither," but the smoothly flowing rhythm used to catch my ear—

> " If youth but knew what age would crave,
> How many a sixpence youth would save ! "

Though the old man himself had not saved much, he possibly might be excused, as his old age—and he lived to be ninety-two—was one that craved but little. His health till the end of his long life was good, and his wants were few. He suffered towards the last, it is true, from a pain to account for which he had to go back seventy-four years, when, as he used to say, he remembered having strained himself in carrying a sack of clover seed, though he had never noticed any effects of it since. He had survived his accident rather longer than an old fellow-parishioner, who died at the age of eighty-eight, seventy-one years after she had been actually " laid forth " as a corpse, having been taken for dead by her attendants in an attack of scarlet fever.

Another of our " ancients " who had every reason to be thankful for the good helpmate whom God had given him, used often to say that in his opinion a thousand pounds " in " a wife was a great deal better than a thousand pounds " with " a wife.

I was struck by an answer of a mother, who once

had got children of all ages about her, and to whom, as she was not strong, I had happened to say—

" I am afraid all these children are a good deal of trouble to you."

" Oh no, sir," she said, " children aren't trouble ; they're only fatigue."

The distinction seemed to me not an unreasonable one, reserving, as it apparently did, the deeper sense of trouble for that brought home too often by sons and daughters no longer children.

Hints on the rearing of children I often get, though not uncommonly on the principle of how not to do it. When I think of the conditions under which many of our poorer children are brought up, I often wonder how they turn out half as well as they do. Given one not over large living-room—the only refuge except the open air for all the various tempers and passions of a father and mother, and six or seven children of all ages and dispositions ; given two bedrooms, from each of which every sound of a crying child or a groaning sick person passes through the thin partition into the next room, and often through the unceiled floor into the living-room ; given even the ordinary worries and irritations of life, aggravated now and then by a little beer, and less money, on Saturday night ; given the not over-soothing effect of an occasional lecture from a clergyman or district visitor, who, judging of things from a cleaner, airier, and more generally comfortable point of view, speaks accordingly ; given all these drawbacks, and many more, and who can be surprised if some poor cottages are not exactly schools of patience, resignation, good temper and refinement ? A word and a blow are a very ready discipline in an area in which no one of its occupants can be very much more than an arm's length from another, and a large part of many children's time is probably spent in simply calculating how often they can do what they like, against orders, after the word, before the blow comes. It must have been a sense of this common experience which made a woman once say to me, in speaking of the superior system on which she herself had been brought up—

" Ah, sir, I'd as good a mother as ever a child need to have. Whatever she promised me I was sure to get it, whether it was a bull's-eye or a hiding."

The certainty of rewards and punishments is an acknowledged element of successful moral training, and the uncertainty of the proportion of actual punishment to the threats of it gives just that excitement of chance to disobedience which is, to many children, an additional incentive to continuance in ill-doing. The word and the blow system, moreover, begets sad callousness both in parents and children. I quite remember being somewhat horrified soon after I came into Sussex by a message which was sent to our schoolmaster by the father of a boy who, having been brought up in this system, would do nothing except through fear of punishment. He became at last so troublesome that he was sent home as beyond the power of our discipline. He was, however, summarily " had back " by an elder brother, who returned him to the master with the message—

" Please, sir, father says you be to take him back, and you be to half kill him."

In spite of this early bringing up the boy has turned out well. I occasionally see a small rod hung up on a cottage wall as a wholesome emblem of authority, but I am inclined to hope that parental violence is decidedly less common among us than it was.

I am thankful to say that work is still a leading idea in the minds of our parents, and education is not yet looked upon simply as a means of " getting by " hard work. The doctrine which a worthy woman propounded to me *apropos* of some relations who had come down in the world still holds its ground.

" To my mind," she said, " it's a deal easier to be brought up to hard work and then to have to leave it off, than it is to be brought up a ' gentleman ' and then to have to take to hard work."

To this same good woman I was indebted for a proverbial rhyme on the subject of family ties, of which, once heard, practical experience reminds us. Speaking of not being able to leave home because of her children, she added—

" It's like the old saying, sir,—

' When you've got one you can run,
    When you've got two you may go,
But when you've got three you must bide where you be.' "

The following rebuke, which I once heard given to an impatient child, had a quaint sound about it : " I should think you stood a good way back when patience was shared out " ; and the way in which people make trouble for themselves when they have nothing else especially to trouble about was also pithily expressed in a saying which I heard not long since—

" Well, Mary, I suppose you are in trouble for the want of trouble."

The commonly accepted doctrine that the two things sufficient to drive a man mad are " a cross wife " and " a smoky chimney " receives a local addition among us of " green wood and no bellows," the force of which is thoroughly understood by any man who gets up early on a dark morning to light a wood fire and boil the kettle before he goes away to work.

May the man who ever feels tempted to madness by any one of these allowedly severe trials take a lesson, nevertheless, from the following instructive narrative, which I have received from one of my parishioners—

A man whose wife was blessed with a remarkably even temper went over the way to a neighbour one evening and said—

" Neighbour, I just should like to see my wife cross for once. I've tried all I know, and I can't make her cross no one way."

" You can't make your wife cross ? " said his neighbour ; " I wish I could make mine anythin' else. But you just do what I tell you, and if that won't act, nothin' will. You bring her in some night a lot of the crookedest bats you can get, them as won't lie in no form, and see how she makes out then." The " bats," or pieces of wood, were accordingly brought in, as awkward and crooked and contrary as could be found. The man went away early to work, and at noon returned to see the result of his experiment. He was greeted with a smiling face and the gentle request—

" Tom, do bring me in some more of those crooked ' bats ' if you can find them ; they did just clip round the kettle nicely."

VI

WHEN I was an undergraduate at Oxford I
was walking behind two boys in the High
Street, and overheard a singular fragment
of their conversation which introduced what seemed
to be a proverbial expression, though it was new to me,
and where the boy got it I have never been able to guess.
One said to the other—

" You're no gentleman ! "

The other at once retorted—

" No gentleman ! I have got wit and manners, and
you've got neither wit, wealth, nor manners ! "

Wit, wealth, and manners struck me as being attri-
butes which describe a gentleman a good deal more
accurately than " keeping a gig," and many other
attempts to define one of the most complex words in
our language. Where a common street-boy got such
a definition I cannot conceive.

The necessity of manners as an element of the
definition of a gentleman was early impressed upon
me by a story of my father's which was current in
his undergraduate days, and which is now probably
seventy years old. A discussion had arisen on the
question—even then by no means a new one—which
of the two Universities was the more gentlemanly
in its general tone and spirit ? It was at length
agreed to refer the decision to a Mr. Besant, then a
very popular " whip " who drove between Oxford and

Cambridge. Mr. Besant flatly refused to arbitrate, on the not unreasonable ground that he was equally kindly received at both Universities. Being, however, at last pressed into compliance, he distinctly gave his judgment in favour of the University of A. His reason being demanded, he at once delivered himself to the following effect—

"Well, gentlemen, if you must have my reason, it is this : I am well known both in A and B, and gentlemen in either University are often kind enough to ask me to their parties. Now, if a gentleman at A wishes to take wine with me he will say—

"'Mr. Besant, may I have the pleasure of a glass of wine with you?'

"But if a gentleman at B wishes to do the same he will say—

"'Besant, my looks towards you,' and that, gentlemen, I call too familiar."

The difficulty, however, of inventing a thoroughly comprehensive definition of this particular character is exemplified by another University story of the same date, and from the same source, which tends to the point that even wit, wealth, and manners are not sufficient, unless manners be taken in the very broad Wykehamical sense implied in the motto, "Manners makyth man." Wit, wealth, and manners in the ordinary sense omit the idea not only of personal honesty, but also of that generous confidence in other people's honesty without which no man, according to the following opinion, is a gentleman. Some undergraduates, talking to a well-known horse-dealer of the day, said rather off-handedly—

"Oh, Smith, how you do take men in about a horse!"

" Take men in, sir, take men in ! What do you mean ? I don't take them in. If a gentleman comes to me and says—

" ' Mr. Smith, I want a good horse ; now you know what a good horse is, so look me out one,' and treats me as one gentleman should treat another, I treats him according. But when I show a horse to a gentleman, if he begins at once—

" ' Why, he's got a spavin, or he's thick in the wind,' and pretends to know something about a horse, why, of course I does him."

My own experience has certainly taught me to believe that on the whole I get better served by throwing myself on the honour of a tradesman in matters of which I can have but little technical knowledge, than many do who know only just enough to make them critical and suspicious. I say " on the whole," because the last silk umbrella which I bought on this principle was certainly not successful.

In connection with this word " gentleman," I have been once or twice not flattered. I remember asking a servant whether she knew who it was that had called while I was out, and I said—

" Was it a clergyman ? "

" Oh no, sir," she replied, " it wasn't a clergyman ; it was a gentleman."

An " old soldier " tramp rather amused me some years ago from the same point of view. He did not straightforwardly beg, but as I passed he said to his mate, quite loudly enough for me to hear—

" Very like Major Beckwith "—I did not respond— " only more of a gentleman."

I was still untouched, and my punishment awaited me.

" The Major I mean," were the last words that caught my ear.

Among our own people the element of living on income without having to do anything for a living forms undoubtedly a large part of the idea of a gentleman, as was once illustrated to me by an inquiry made of a man who was out of work by a more fortunate neighbour—

" Well, Bill, how long have you been ' gentleman ' ? "

At one of the Club feasts in our parish, some time ago, I had sung a song written before 1830, and still popular, called " A Thousand a Year," and I well remember the remark of one of the labouring men in the audience—

" Well, if I'd got a thousand a year I shouldn't do much work ; it would take me all my time to spend it."

Fortunately, however, freedom from the necessity of work is not the whole of the idea, for a poor man who had received a kindness under somewhat onerous conditions from a person whose wealth and leisure were unquestionable, once sadly complained to me—

" I don't like dealing with your half-bred gentlemen."

It has not often been my lot to hear poor people say much about the blessings of a poor estate. The not unnatural longing of toilers is rather for that haven of rest and freedom from care which they connect with the idea of wealth ; and a poor woman once apologized to me for some shortcomings incident to her condition in life, in what sounded at the time very typical words—

" Ah, sir, poverty doesn't show our best side."

One of our village oracles, whom I remember, used to say—

" Poverty's no sin, but it's precious inconvenient.'

The poor man in his early days had had plenty to keep him in comfort, but having lived on the principle of a somewhat Johnsonian definition attributed to one of his compeers that " enough is just a little more than ever a man can make away with," he had come to want.

I often, however, called to mind an utterance from an opposite point of view of one of my poorer parishioners, whom I used to take with me when I drove anywhere at night, and with whom I had from time to time considerable opportunities of conversation One evening, in the course of our talk, he said :

" Well, sir, in my opinion, a working man who likes work, and who has got work to go to, when he comes home at night ought to be one of the happiest men alive, if he ain't afeared of being took for nothin'."

This last curiously qualifying clause, which seemed to suggest that the fear of being " took " for something was not unusual among working men, gave a new turn to my inquiries, which resulted in the good man asserting for himself, at all events, complete faith in the doctrine that honesty is the best policy. This proverb, however, he paraphrased to the following effect—

" Good principles, sir, good principles, yes, they be the things ; I hold wi' them. Somethin' allus turns up as makes them pay."

Proverbs are naturally the form which much of our native wisdom takes, and occasionally I meet with one which is quite new to me. A cottager was telling me lately that her husband and herself had lived for

wenty-three years in their present cottage, and that
er husband had worked on the same farm longer still,
nd she added—

"And I don't know but what we've been foolish for
topping in one place as long as we have done. People
ay we have, anyhow."

I quoted the very obvious proverb, "A rolling stone
athers no moss," to which she replied at once—

"Yes, sir, and a sitting hen gets no feathers."

I felt that I had taken little by my suggestion.
When I was a growing lad I used to deprecate the
stonishment of a kindly old farmer's wife, who saw
e at intervals of about six months, by saying in all
imility—

"Ill weeds grow apace."

"Yes," she would answer, "and good rye thrives
gh."

Proverbs somehow seem nearly to balance each
her, and a good memory would generally be able, I
agine, to furnish one exactly opposite to any one
at might be quoted.

The following quaint saying I have heard used among
to express the not uncommon occurrence of the
ad of a family being able to introduce various
embers of the family into the same employ—

'Yes, sir, the fingers have got pretty close to the
umb."

Not long ago I was a good deal touched by the
ilosophy, which I wish was proverbial, of a poor
man, who, speaking of Sunday, said to me—

'I have a hard matter to make both ends meet all
week, but on Sunday I never trouble ; I leave it
to God that day."

Knowing what her struggle for existence is, and

how it is made more severe by weak health and a
large family, I am convinced that this cessation from
worry and anxiety on one day out of the seven,
coupled, as it is, with a distinct act of faith in God, is
of the greatest use in helping her to maintain the
battle of life—as, indeed, she does maintain it—most
bravely.

For the following items of conversation I claim
nothing more than the piquancy given to expressions
by the unexpected form which they take. Some
years ago I paid a visit, after a long absence, to my
birthplace in Cheshire. One of the first persons upon
whom I happened to call was a shoemaker, of whom
when I was a boy, I used to see a good deal. Since we
had last met I had, of course, considerably developed,
and I was no longer the stripling whom he remembered.
I looked in through the " side-door " into the shop
and said—

" Well, William, how are you ? "

He looked up, pushed his spectacles on to his forehead, and, after a pause, made no more direct answer
to my greeting than—

" Eh, mester ; but it's a grand country yo coom
from somewheer."

Our Sussex equivalent would have been that "
did credit to my keep."

On another visit, some years later, I called again,
when, among other questions, he asked—

" Well, mester, and how's the missus ? "

I answered—

" What's the good of asking that, William ? Why,
I'm not married ! "

" And you're in th' reet [right] on't," was the
prompt but unfeeling reply.

BODLE HOLMES, A CENTENARIAN NATIVE OF HEATHFIELD, 1885

The physical development which struck him was once also a bar to my recognition as curate in my new parish in London. I was introducing myself to my parishioners, and I had done so to a small tradesman who was standing at the door of his shop. After a little talk he called to his wife, who was busy at the back of the shop—

"Mary, this is the new curate."

"Oh! I beg the gentleman's pardon," was the response; "I didn't think he was fine-draw'd enough for a curate."

My rector happened to be considerably less in bulk than myself, and the good woman thought, I suppose, that, be a rector what he might, he ought to be bigger than a curate. Size evidently does enter into some people's calculations of clerical correctness. A friend of mine, a country clergyman, very tall and of a distinctly dignified appearance, had been away from his parish for a holiday. On his return he inquired, with a little natural anxiety, how his substitutes had acquitted themselves.

"Oh, well there, sir," was the answer, "they did pretty middlin' answerable to their size; but, you know, sir, if I may make so bold, *you* are the King of the Cannibal Islands."

In a little shop a few doors lower down the street which my London parishioner was so sceptical, occupied at the time of which I am speaking by a working watchmaker, I once picked up a hint as to the sad uses to which the study of human nature is occasionally put. A man happened to be in the shop who was employed in "black work"—or who, in other words, worked for an undertaker—and in saying something about his occupation I remember that he made what sounded to me a cruel statement.

" Yes, sir," he said, " it's a rule in our trade that if you want to get your money easy you must send the bill in while the tears is in the eyes."

There is no reason whatever, so far as I know, to suppose that undertakers are less tender-hearted than other men, and I took the utterance to mean merely that, under the influence of strong emotions, either of sorrow or of joy, people are less disposed to raise questions and disputes than they might be in quieter moments. It is only now and then that I find a bridegroom inclined to grumble in the vestry at the amount of the marriage fee, whereas if he were applied to a week later he might happen to be very captious.

But to leave St. Mary Axe and its associations, and return to human nature in its rural aspect.

Shepherds are commonly credited with a good deal of wisdom, the result of much solitary and independent thinking ; but the life of the shepherd of poetry is a very different one from that of the modern shepherd, whose sole business is to bring forward his sheep as fast as possible for the butcher.

A hill-shepherd in Scotland, who is not engaged from morning to night in hurdle-pitching, turnip-cutting, and other matter-of-fact work, may meditate and cultivate wisdom, but in our south country shepherds are much like other men, as far as my experience goes. Once, I confess, I picked up a theory from a Wiltshire shepherd which might have pleased Mr. Darwin. I happened to ask my friend why shepherds set so much store by sheep-dogs without tails. The question was apparently new, and the good man did not answer at once. At last he said—

" Well, sir, I do think they be truer bred to sit like."

The following piece of shepherd wisdom I have only had told me, and if it is in print I can only say that I have never seen it. When it was told me, Sir Isaac Newton was made the subject of it, but the point is not lost by the substitution of any other philosopher. Sir Isaac was riding over the downs, pondering deeply over something else than the weather. An old shepherd whom he passed said—

" If you don't want to get wet, sir, you'd better make haste home."

Sir Isaac looked up at the sky, but saw no sign of a storm, and thanking the man, rode slowly away. The man again advised him to mend his pace. In about a quarter of an hour down came a thunder-plump and wetted Sir Isaac to the skin. He immediately turned his horse, rode back to the shepherd, and offered him a shilling if he would tell him how he knew the rain was coming.

The shepherd at once enlightened him.

" D'ye see thik [1] old sheep ? " pointing to one of his flock.

" Yes," said Sir Isaac.

" Well, then," said the man, " whenever you do see thik old sheep turn his tail to the wind you may be sure it's going to rain."

What Sir Isaac thought of his " wether " glass the story did not say.

I have learnt many a lesson of good management in our cottages which might satisfy the most careful Scot. One thoroughly good manager I prevailed upon some years ago to give me details, as nearly as she could,

[1] Pure Wiltshire for " that."

of the weekly spending of a weekly income of 15s. 6d.
It took the following form :—

		s.	d.
Rent	. . . .	2	0
7 gallons of flour	. . . . .	7	0
2 lb. of Dutch cheese	. . . .	1	3
1 lb. of butter	. . . . .	1	4
½ lb. of soap	. . . . .	0	2
Soda ½d., blue ½d.	. . . . .	0	1
Salt and pepper	. . . . .	0	0½
1½ lb. of candles	. . . . .	0	10½
2 oz. of tea	. . . . . .	0	4
2 lb. of sugar	. . . . .	0	7
Schooling	. . . . . .	0	7
Cotton 1d., mustard, etc., 2d.	. . . .	0	3
Milk per week, viz. ¼ of a pint of skim daily		0	3½
Mangling	. . . . . .	0	1
	Total .	14	10½

Outgoings for wood, clothing, boots, shoes, and other
items not included in the above balance-sheet, are
defrayed from extra earnings by piecework, woodcutting, mowing, harvest, hopping, and hop-drying.

The good management lay in getting out of these
materials more comfort for a family consisting of husband, wife, and six children, the eldest aged fourteen,
than many housekeepers would get out of nearly double
the income. One great difficulty is, so to manage that
the living shall be about the same on Friday and Saturday as it is on Sunday and Monday. "A feast and a
fast," as our folk say, is not an uncommon system with
bad managers, whereas forethought and a clear head
will naturally greatly lessen this evil. I have tried,
but in vain, to persuade my informant to write down
for me from time to time the various little recipes by

which she gives variety and piquancy to the simple substances on which she has to feed the family. If I could only remember the devices that have frequently surprised me by their ingenuity, I should be able to compile a little handbook of cottage economy, for which the authorities at South Kensington would, I believe, thank me.

The failures of well-meant attempts on the part of amateur economists to assist the poor in the art of management once met with a rebuke which amused our people when it happened long ago, and which is not yet forgotten. A lady, whose earnest desire to do good was well known in this neighbourhood, had persuaded an undoubtedly bad manager to let her have for once the laying out of the week's money. Having carefully considered what was most needed for the family, she went to the shop, and having returned, laid forth upon the cottage table the things she had bought, giving the woman at the same time some trifling change, and saying—

" There, friend, I think you will allow that I have spent your money to rather better advantage than you sometimes do yourself."

" Oh, thank you, ma'am," said the woman ; " but where's the grist ? "

All the money had gone in " shop things," and the largest item of outlay, viz. the flour, the good lady had utterly overlooked.

It was just such a manager as the one this lady tried to help, of whom one of our shopkeepers told me, after she had gone with her family to America, that he had lost at any rate a steady customer, for that she regularly came or sent for a quarter of an ounce of penny tea, that is a farthing's worth, four times a day.

When I asked what her reason could be for not giving an order for at least a whole pennyworth at once, he said that she had no doubt noticed that he did not weigh out the quarter of an ounce, but guessed it, and that so probably she had calculated on getting a little more by taking an ounce at four times than if she had taken it all at once.

Had I been set to guess her reason I should have been a long time guessing this, but I make little question that it was the right one. While I am on the subject of domestic management I may quote a recipe for avoiding family quarrels, which I think may fairly claim credit for good sense. It was given me by an old man as invented and practised by a couple whom he used to know, down " Chidding-lye " way.

" You see, sir," he said, " they'd agreed between themselves that whenever he came home a little ' contrary,' and out of temper, he wore his hat on the back of his head, and then she never said a word ; and if she came in a little ' crass ' and crooked, she threw her shawl over her left shoulder, and then he never said a word."

If similarly wise danger-signals could be pretty largely used, how many unnecessary collisions would be avoided, and how many a long train of evil consequences would be safely shunted till the line was clear again ! This self-denying reticence stands, however, I fear, in singular contrast with the " hot supper " which often awaits the husband whose coming home depends more upon " turning-out time "—the time, that is, when our public-houses are cleared and closed—than upon care for the peace and quiet of his family.

VII

IN some interesting papers on Old Marriage Customs published in the "Leisure Hour," Mr. Thiselton Dyer derives from ancient Rome many of the marriage observances which were quite common in England within the last century. In his chapter on Roman Marriage Customs he begins with the preliminary stage of matrimony, viz. the betrothal or engagement, which he tells us was regarded quite as a solemn act, and was attended with various ceremonies. Here he starts with a clear advantage over any one who undertakes to describe Sussex marriage customs within the last century. We do not wish to underrate the solemnity of the act of betrothal on the part of Sussex young men and maidens, but the various ceremonies connected with the act have not been reduced to such a uniform system as to admit of precise description. Inasmuch, however, as we have never heard of the betrothals or engagements of our young people being prevented, or even seriously hindered, by ignorance of the proper ceremonies, we imagine that our young folk, with their native independence, invent ceremonies for themselves. The ceremonies doubtless vary according to the nature of the case and the temperament of the inventors, but at any rate they are sufficient for the purpose. On this point, therefore, we must yield to the Romans, as we have little to say.

The Romans, however, in their turn, must fairly

yield to us in another preliminary of marriage, viz.
the publication of banns. They could not have had,
I am sure, any ceremony at all equivalent to that to
which I used to listen with doubtful interest forty
years ago in St. Pancras Church, in London, when
probably five minutes were occupied every Sunday
morning in a monotonous gabble of " Also between
Thomas Brown, bachelor, and Mary Ann Green,
spinster, both of this parish," and thirty or forty
more bachelors and spinsters, utterly unknown to
every member of the congregation. In country
churches where the persons " asked " are better known
to their fellow-parishioners, an occasional interest is
given to the ceremony of " asking " by the forbidding
of the banns. I have never myself heard banns
forbidden, but a friend has told me that on the day
on which his own banns were published in a church
in Scotland the names also of another couple were
proclaimed, whereupon a shrill voice was heard to
declare from the other end of the building, " I winna
hae that marriage of James Lowrie." I gathered
also from my friend that after service a young woman
was seen in the vestry accepting as a compensation
for slighted affections the exact sum of seven shillings
and sixpence. I have often wondered how such a
precise amount could have been arrived at as a
satisfaction for a broken heart, but it has sometimes
occurred to me that possibly the rejected maiden
might have demanded ten shillings, and that the
half-crown was the largest abatement from the sum
asked to which she would submit.

Our own parish church has, however, been the wit-
ness within the memory of man, not, it is true, of a
forbidding of banns, but of an attempt to prevent the

marriage ceremony itself, which, as an instance of persistency on the part of a rejected admirer, has, I imagine, been rarely surpassed. The disappointed suitor followed the young woman and his more fortunate rival into the church, addressing the bride-elect from time to time in piteous tones, " Say ' No,' Martha ; say ' No,' Martha " ; and this he continued till the crucial question was put, " Wilt thou have this man to thy wedded husband ? " As soon as the fatal words, " I will," had passed the bride's lips instead of the " No," which he had fondly hoped for, he turned away and left the church.

In connection with the publication of banns I have heard from a brother clergyman an incident, the truth of which internal evidence may be said to guarantee, inasmuch as it seems beyond the power of invention. The good old minister of whom it was told always used to have the book containing the banns put on the reading-desk just at his right hand. One Sunday morning he began as usual, " I publish the banns of marriage between——" and putting down his hand in all confidence for the book, found to his dismay that it was not there. In his nervousness, while searching for the missing register, he kept on repeating the formula, " I publish the banns of marriage between—— I publish the banns of marriage between——" till at last the clerk from beneath, in sheer pity, came to the rescue, with a suggestion whispered loudly enough to be heard all over the church, " between the cushion and the desk, sir." The book had simply slipped under the cushion ; the result of the accident was a publication of banns which I should imagine to be unique.

Among our less educated folk there still lingers a

superstition that it is unlucky for young people to hear their own banns published, for fear lest their firstborn child should be deaf and dumb ; but though it fell to my lot even to publish my own banns, no evil consequences have ensued. One difficulty connected with this preliminary ceremony is undoubtedly that of residence. It seems clearly understood that during the " asking " the persons " asked " should reside in the parish in which they are " asked " ; but when the question arises, " What is residence ? " ideas become very hazy and indefinite. Hiring a room for the time is looked upon, I imagine, as ample compliance with the law, quite independently of any occupation of the room ; but a stocking or a glove left in a friend's cottage is, I fear, not unfrequently held to justify its owner in asserting residence, or the friend in asserting residence, for the owner.

Unhappily, however, legal fictions are in many ways so common, that such an one as this is not considered by any means a serious instance of the kind.

The Marriage Service itself used to be far more productive of scenes than it is now, and education is doing much to secure outward decorum, at any rate during the ceremony. Occasionally, however, still one's nerves are sorely taxed by things said and done under the combined influence of nervousness, ignorance, and shyness. I did not argue much good from the preliminary questions of a " hopper," who stopped me in the village street one Saturday evening after dark, and said—

" Please, sir, can you ask me twice one Sunday ? " —meaning, I suppose, at morning and afternoon service both.

" No, friend," I replied, " I can't do that."

Then, after a pause—

" Please, sir, can you marry me the same Sunday I'm asked out ? " was his next inquiry.

I was obliged, of course, to say that I could not accommodate him even in this way.

" But," I added, " what makes you in such a hurry ? "

" Well, you see, sir," he said, " we're hoppers, and we don't want to be stopping about here after hops are done."

I agreed to marry them at eight o'clock on the Monday morning after they were " out-asked," and they accordingly presented themselves. All went well for a time, till suddenly the bridegroom put his head between his hands, began to cry, and walked away to the other end of the church. The bride did not look as much surprised as I should have expected, and the groomsman, another huge " hopper," seemed barely surprised at all. Seeing, however, that his mate showed no signs of coming back, he turned half round, and called out with a loud voice—

" Come, Joe, be a man ; stand up like a man, Joe."

Upon this Joe slowly returned and stood up and said what was necessary. He went away again, but not till the essential part of the service was finished. After the service I asked the clerk what the meaning of this behaviour was. I thought it must have been that the man was worse for drink, but the explanation was that he had not long buried his first wife, and that he was overcome by his feelings.

A friend of mine in the next parish but one told me some years ago of a wedding experience which happened to him, and in which I sincerely hope that he kept his countenance. The couple being married was a specially rustic one ; it was the winter-time and the bridegroom had a bad cold ; he had managed with a sad snuffle to say the words in a fashion after the clergyman till the betrothal ; but then, having both hands occupied in holding the ring on the bride's finger, and fearing probably that if he let go he should invalidate the ceremony, he felt the coming difficulty, and so, while waiting to be " taught by the priest," instead of beginning, " With this ring I thee wed," he turned round to his groomsman, and said, in the most matter-of-fact voice—

" Wipe my noase for me, will 'ee, Bill ? "

Latterly, however, as I have already said, I have rarely had any reason to be nervous about the conduct of persons who come to be married. I have noticed that the woman is generally better prepared with the responses and other particulars of the service than the man, though the difficulty of giving the right hand seems the greater with the woman ; and the combinations of left with right, left with left, right with left, are often exhausted before right meets right. The reason I have imagined to be that the woman comes to church so impressed with the necessity of offering the left hand for the ring, that the preliminary need of the right hand confuses her. However, in the vestry the woman is often triumphant, and writes her name when the man is content with a mark. Sussex, indeed, in respect of women's signatures in the marriage register, has, I believe, for many years stood second among all the counties in England.

But apart from the particular instance of the marriage ceremony, in few things is the difference between old and new Sussex more marked than in matters connected with our churches and church services. Isolated as our parishes are, undisturbed as they used to be by any public opinion other than that which existed within their own borders, accustomed as they were to their own clergyman, and with rare exceptions to him only, things were said and done by clergymen and by parish clerks in former days, and done without attracting any special notice, which would now immediately furnish paragraphs for the local newspapers, and through them for newspapers all over the kingdom. I once myself heard a Sussex clerk, in the service for the Queen's Accession, take upon himself to substitute, as more suitable for the occasion, the words, " And blessed be the name of her Majesty for ever, and all the earth shall be filled with her Majesty," for the original words of the Psalmist.

In these days of organs, harmoniums, and choirs, I am not likely again to have the following experience. I was doing duty one hot summer afternoon in a part of Sussex where I had never taken the service before. Our music was a clarionet, which for some reason or other, in the third verse of the hymn, ceased to play, and left the singers to themselves. When service was over, I happened to inquire the cause of the stoppage, and was told—

" Well, there, sir, the poor man he be forced to stop, he do perspire so."

He had simply put down his instrument to wipe his face.

The following is from West Sussex : Many years ago there lived in that part of the county a nobleman who was very fond of animals of all kinds, and among his lordship's pets was a tame wolf. Early one Sunday morning a servant came in to say that the wolf

seemed very ill. His lordship, not knowing what else
to do, sent off a groom at once with a note to a
neighbouring clergyman, who was noted for his skill
in treating all diseases of dumb animals, asking him
to come over and see the wolf as soon as he could.
The clergyman, so the story goes—and I have heard
the story told in such very different quarters that I
think there must be at least a foundation of truth in
it—gave some instructions to his clerk. These instructions the worthy clerk very possibly translated into
the language which he thought likely to be best
" understanded of the people " ; but, at any rate, before
the last hymn at Morning Prayer, he made the following announcement to the congregation—

" I hereby give notice that there won't be no service
in this church this afternoon, 'cause master's gooin'
to bleed his lordship's 'oolf."

A share of this good clergyman's veterinary skill
would have prevented much suffering on the part of
a poor Indian cow with the orthodox hump, which
was some years ago sent over from the East to a
friend of my own. My friend, wishing to know how
the animal was going on, wrote to inquire of the farm
bailiff who had charge of it. The answer was " that
they hoped the cow was better, but that in coming
down in the train she had catched a hurt, which had
rose a hump on her back ; they had been ' doctering ' it
ever since, and they hoped it had gone down—a little."

But this by the way, and with an apology to parish
clerks for the digression.

The parish clerk of the following paragraph was not
a Sussex man, it is true, though he lived only a few
miles across the Kentish border. It was, however,
from a Sussex man, who was present in church at

the time, that my informant, a Robertsbridge neighbour, got the story.

The old clerk set the hymns, managed the singing, and worked the barrel-organ. He was, however, so partial to the " Old Hundredth," that in an evil hour the clergyman asked him if he could not now and then give them another tune, and if it wasn't on the barrel whether he couldn't set it with a pitch-pipe. The old man didn't say much at the time, but evidently felt deeply this interference with his authority as master of the music, and accordingly at the next singing he gave out—

" Let us sing to the praise and glory of God, the hundred and nineteenth psalm, *from eend to eend* " (176 verses).

Our own late clerk used to tell me of a curious incident, which he himself well remembered. A child is entered in our register baptized in the names " Samuel Orange " as Christian names. This, he said, was a compromise, the names desired by the sponsors being " Oranges and Lemons." The curate, however, resisted, on the not unreasonable ground that ' Oranges and Lemons " were not Christian names. A consultation was held, but the curate was firm, and ' Samuel Orange " were the names eventually given.

Our parish clerk and sexton aforesaid, whose direct ancestors had held these offices since 1728, had in his own day witnessed many changes of manners and customs connected with the church and churchyard. He had himself, he told me, kept watch for two nights over the grave of a man who had died of some disease sufficiently unusual to have attracted a party of body-snatchers from a distance, with a view of procuring an interesting subject for the dissecting-room. Nor was this the only instance, even within the memory of man, of the appointment of a " body-guard " to protect the grave of a parishioner who had had the misfortune to die of some other than a commonplace ailment. In our churchwardens' accounts as long ago as 1675, I find a charge for " watching the church " when a Mr. Cason was buried, but what this watching was for is not said. In the same year there is an item of 1s. 6d. " expended in numbering the people," a charge certainly not exorbitant, if the population was anything like the 2285 of which it consisted in 1881. I do not know that extracts from the parochial accounts of a wild country parish, when those accounts are not more than two hundred years old, can be very interesting to extra-parochial readers. I think, however, that from our books I can produce an instance of fixity of prices, at any rate as regards the nominal amount, which has possibly escaped the notice of political economists and statisticians. In 1676 the parish, " for washing the surplice three times "—possibly before the " three times at least " administration of the Holy Communion—paid three shillings. In 1876 the incumbent for each washing of the surplice paid 1s., so that for two hundred years the charge, nominally at least, has been stationary. The vicar's dinner at the visitation in those days cost 2s., and the parish paid for it—a fact the recurrence of which I own that I cannot personally call " a recol lection," but those were times in which the destruction of foxes at 1s., and of hedgehogs at 2d. a head, " whip ping disorderly boys and dogs during Divine service " at 20s. per annum, and various other charges, were uncomplainingly borne by the church-rate. Wha accident rendered an hour-glass for the pulpit neces

sary twice in four years I cannot say, but the charge
for each was 8d. In our list of customary fees, dated
1750, I find the entry of a 10s. fee for an ordinary
funeral sermon—an entry followed by the somewhat
singular addition : " Text chosen by friends of de-
ceased," £1. This extra payment assumed, I suppose,
that a fresh text might involve the preacher in the
labour of a fresh sermon—an admission which bespoke
probably small hope of novelty for 10s. I can only
trust that 10s. funeral sermons were more effective
than a farewell sermon which I preached on leaving
my London curacy, and which I wrote for that
occasion only, and to which a parishioner alluded a
day or two afterwards in the touching words—

" Ah, sir, I heard your farewell sermon—and I—
nearly shod a tear."

Our district is, I think I may say, essentially
Puritan in its Church views. The Mayfield burnings
during the Marian persecution are not yet forgotten,
and a cottager in my own parish is daily reminded
of them by a " fireback " which faces him every time
he looks to his fire. These " firebacks " are plates of
iron placed behind our " down " fires, or fires on the
hearth, to keep the brands from the wall and to throw
out the heat. These plates, cast in olden days at our
local forges, have on them occasionally very quaint
devices, and on the one of which I am now speaking
here are the figures of a man and woman chained
back to back to a stake, and surrounded by most
palpable cast-iron flames. What wonder if the owner
of such an historical record should be inclined, however unreasonably, to visit the sins of the fathers
upon the children, and to feel that the less any form
of religion has in common with the one to whose

deeds of more than three hundred years ago his iron plate testifies, the truer it must be ? It must be added that the ideas of our people about the Church of Rome are as a rule most vague. One good old body, whom I knew well, having received a visit from the wife of a bishop of our Church who was staying in the parish, took great pains to inform her friends that " the Pope's wife " had been to see her. Another good Protestant cottager, evidently ill-informed on the subject of " Catholicism," said to me one day—

" A curious sort of religion, sir, this Catholic religion, isn't it ? They tell me that a man keeps ' pooking ' [i.e. pushing] a lot of beads over his shoulder while the parson keeps all on a-preaching."

Without entering upon the question of the creed or other tests of " Catholicity," I was at any rate able to assure him that his views of the " Catholic religion " were, to say the least, inadequate.

VIII

MISCONCEPTIONS, however, extend to matters of less interest than faith and discipline. Some years ago a Roman Catholic lady lived for a time on the confines of our parish. One of our girls was in her service, but having left it, was magnifying to her new mistress her late employer's wealth, and by way of giving one instance out of many, she said—

" Oh yes, ma'am, she was very rich ; I do assure you, ma'am, that all her flannel petticoats were made of silk."

Nor are we in our turn exempt from being misunderstood even by members of our own communion as well as by those who differ from us. Till lately it was our custom for the clergyman, when officiating, to wear "bands," but my indifference to them was somewhat increased, and my inclination to give them up strengthened, by one of my singing boys, as he saw me searching for them one Sunday morning in the vestry, asking me whether I was looking for my "bib." When, in obedience, as I believed, to a celebrated judgment of the House of Lords, I left off the use of the gown in preaching, I was not a little amused by the question put to a lady parishioner by a good woman, a Nonconformist, who asked in perfect good faith—

" What's all this fuss, miss, about our parson and his white pinafore ? "

This ignorance of the technicalities of clerical dress is quite independent of respect for the clerical character, and I can hardly imagine any class of people more ready and willing than our Sussex folk are to recognize the work of a clergyman who does his duty among them earnestly and with a reasonable amount of common sense. There is, no doubt, a certain degree of traditional respect for the mere office of the clergyman ; but this has to be fortified by a personal respect for the individual clergyman as an ambassador of Christ before it becomes a really abiding sentiment in an East Sussex man's breast. Of the traditional element of respect I was once unexpectedly reminded while I was a curate in London. I had sent for the son of one of my late parishioners to come up to town, as I thought that I could get him a place. While I was walking with him through the City to call at a business house where I hoped to get him in, he was very silent, but he was evidently being struck with the small amount of recognition which I received in the streets as compared with what used to be the case in Sussex, for at last he mustered courage, and said—

" They don't seem to make much account of parsons up here, sir."

Of late, however—as far, at least, as the younger part of our community is concerned—London and the country are becoming much more on a par on this point. The old civility is now, I fear, looked upon by a good many as mere servility ; and occasionally the distinction between independence and impudence is apparently not very accurately understood. I am not, however, in the least degree complaining, as I do not for a moment believe that the withholding the old marks of courtesy means any studied disrespect either to myself or to my office. It arises, I believe, solely from a somewhat mistaken view on the part of our young people of the respect which they owe to themselves and to their manhood ; and I am certainly not without hope that as time goes on some of the present " Mordecais in my gate " will take kindlier views of the relations between us. When I remember the way in which many of my contemporaries at school and college have falsified in after-life the evil expectations formed of them as boys and under-graduates—and by no means always unreasonably formed—by masters and tutors, I cannot lose heart about some of my own young parishioners whose tempers and dispositions as yet do not seem especially amiable.

I well recollect once walking with the good clergy-man who preceded me in this parish, and passing close by a man who, keeping his hands well down in his pockets, took no other notice whatever of the Rector than staring him hard in the face. The Rector, fearing that there might be some cause for the man's seemingly studied rudeness, and thinking that perhaps he might unconsciously have given him some offence, spoke, and the answer he received was an extempore text—

" It says in the Bible, ' Thou shalt not worship man.' "

The Rector, not wishing to enter into any discussion then, passed on, but sent his sturdy parishioner after-wards some quotations from the Book to which he had appealed, showing that there is nothing especially unscriptural in a parishioner recognizing his clergy-man. Whether the good man saw any reason to change his views I do not know, as he shortly afterwards migrated into Kent, and has never returned to the parish.

Whoever may have taken the trouble to read thus far will probably have formed an opinion that our people are of a somewhat matter-of-fact rather than superstitious temperament ; and this is the case. Our local superstitions are few, and a ghost would be very strictly tested before it was allowed to pass as a genuine spirit-manifestation. I once asked in our school, " What is a ghost ? " a question to which one of the boys made answer: "Something what somebody imagines." I have reason to suppose that the idea was not altogether his own ; still, it very fairly expressed our local opinion on the subject. I do not remember having ever heard more than two ghost-stories connected with our parish, and they are told of days long gone by. Indeed, they are in one sense interesting, inasmuch as they are an instance of the length of time which may be covered by a tradition involving only one person between ourselves and the very actor in the scene. My informant is an old parishioner now (1882) alive at the age of eighty-seven. Her grandfather, from whom she received the story, was born in 1737, and died and was buried in our churchyard in 1817. The affair with the ghost happened to him when he was about seventeen years old, or one hundred and twenty-eight years ago.

Not wishing to lose such an instance as this of the possibilities of tradition, I one day found a good easy carriage for my old friend, and having found her also a driver over eighty years of age, and, singularly enough, a horse more than forty years old, I took her down to the National School. She there told her

story in the hearing of the assembled children. I
have kept the names of all present, so that if any of
the children of ten years of age, then in the room,
themselves live to be as old as the old lady, viz.
eighty-seven, they will, at the end of their life, that
is in 1959, be able to say that they were told by a
person who got it from the lips of the very man himself, of something done by a man who was born in
1737—or 222 years before.

Richard Balcombe, the young man in question, had
newly gone to live as servant at " The Greenwoods," a
farmhouse in a very wild district on the south-western
border of our parish. He was sent late one night
with a message to Burwash, and he was warned before
he started that a ghost was very often seen near a
stile which he had to cross. He accordingly took
with him a middling thick stick, and said that if any
ghost interrupted him he would, by the help of his
" bat," try and find out what a ghost was made of.

As he got near to the stile, he duly caught sight of
the ghost in front of him, glaring fiercely out of the
hedge. He put down his basket, walked quietly up
to the place, and with his " bat " struck out boldly.
He owned that he then felt a good deal frightened,
for no sooner had he struck than flames on all sides
came flying past his head. However, he held his
ground, and then discovered that he had smashed into
a hundred pieces an old rotten tree-stump which had
dried up into touchwood, and the phosphorus in
which shone with such mysterious brightness in the
dark. A second ghost gave him more trouble. As
he was going home one night from Burwash with
a pair of half-boots which had been mended, he
suddenly, at a stile again, came face to face with a

ghost. Without more ado, he flung the boots at it. All at once the field seemed filled with ghosts, which jumped up and rushed away. The one which he had seen was an old grey horse which had been standing with its tail to the stile. The boots fell across the horse's back; the horse kicked up its heels in fright; the boots slid on to its shoulders, where they rode safely enough, and though the ghost had vanished it had taken the boots with it.

The following instance of mixed ideas about this world and another, I look upon as very exceptional, though it comes to me from the tradesman who was serving the funeral in Newark parish, at which it occurred. In the ordinary course, he asked the woman who was attending the funeral party for the registrar's certificate of death.

" Do you mean the ticket, sir ? " she said.

" Yes," he replied ; " the ticket."

" Oh, sir ! " said the woman, " I put that in the box [i.e. the coffin] ; I thought the poor soul might want it when he got to heaven."

I should have been curious to trace the origin of this idea, as it has no parallel in my Sussex experience. I have never actually known more than one person who complained of being " overlooked," and I do not think that she had any idea who was the cause of her trouble. I have heard of one man who believing himself to be bewitched, met his tormentor, an old man who lived not far off, coming from a lonesome barn in the shape of a calf ; but the story is indistinct, and I could not make very much of it. I remember one poor woman telling me that, a few nights before, she had seen the Evil One sitting at the foot of her bed. She spoke, and he came nearer to her. She did not quail, but boldly challenged him, and said—

"Come on ; I'll have a brish [brush] wi' you."

She then began to say the Lord's Prayer, and he disappeared.

We have no haunted houses, and as a public foot-path crosses the churchyard, our people are too familiar with the spot to associate it with ghosts and apparitions. In the parish in which I was born in Cheshire, there was a large pool, in part overhung with trees, which as a child I never passed without a certain sense of awe, as I had always heard that every night at twelve o'clock a coach and six horses, with a headless driver, appeared on its banks. We have no similar terrors in this parish.

Even our faith in charms, and other than orthodox methods of curing disease, is waning. A potato carried in the pocket for a certain length of time has been considered a specific for rheumatism. I under-took to put the doctrine to the test myself once, and I promised the good woman who gave me the potato a bushel if it cured me. I carried it till it got almost as hard as wood, but without much effect. I laid it by for a time through forgetfulness, and on taking it again I found that unluckily it had sprouted, so that possibly its virtue was diminished by reason of the sprouts ; and I may be considered, perhaps, not to have given the remedy a fair trial. Two persons at least I know who distinctly affirm that they carried a potato, and that their rheumatism left them. They will not yield as to these two facts ; the connec-tion of cause and effect they leave to the learned. Curiously nasty mixtures are occasionally given to children for measles and other childish complaints, but they are hardly worth the dignity of print. I have known a person who went a long distance to have a live snake applied to the throat for goître; and I have known of a servant-girl who tried the virtue of a dead one for the same ailment, but having worn the charm till it was no longer wearable, it was discovered, and on being obliged to throw it away, she said that if she could not have the dead snake she would go somewhere and get a " dead man's hand " put to her neck. The following cure for ague is vouched to me by one of my most trustworthy parishioners as having been much relied on within his own knowledge: A piece of the nail of each of the patient's fingers and toes is cut off, as well as a bit of hair from the " nod " (i.e. the nape of the neck). They must be taken without the patient's knowledge, that is, while he is asleep, and when this is accomplished they must be wrapped up in a piece of paper, and " the ague," which they represent, must be put into a hole in an " apsen " (i.e. aspen) tree, and be left there, when by degrees the ague will leave the sufferer. The connection of the ague with the aspen tree is an anticipation of homœopathy which may interest some of the disciples of that system. Occasionally the treatment fails, in which case " the ague " must be taken out of the tree, or the malady will continue; and my informant once actually saw a man come and unstop the hole in which he had deposited his son's ague, and carry the ague away.

Our recreations are not very varied. Perhaps the most real pleasure that we have is a good rabbit-hunt. An East Sussex man dearly loves a day with the beagles, and, little as I know about sport, I fully share the sense of exhilaration produced on a clear, bright winter day by the voices of the busy little animals ringing in our woods. The hold which the love of this particular form of enjoyment has upon some of our people was vividly brought before me some years ago, in a conversation with a man who, by this and other means, had wasted a fair income and had come to poverty. I was asking him whether it was true, as it was reported of him—that he was in the habit of saying that if he had his time over again he would live just as he had done.

" Oh no, sir," he replied ; " I never said any such thing as that ; but I have said that if I had my time to come over again, I would keep a ' cry of dogs.' "

Fox-hunting is little known among us. The quantity of " shaws " and woods unfits this part of the country for a good run, and it is said that the only fox which has ever been killed in this parish by hounds was a three-legged one which had been caught in a trap. And yet our parish has been the scene of the finish of one of the most remarkable runs recorded in the history of fox-hunting. I had often heard the tradition of a fox being found in a field just to the north of the village, dead of exhaustion, with a hound, also dead of exhaustion, lying a few yards behind it ; a second hound lying exhausted, though still alive, not far off. The tradition always pointed to Salisbury Plain as the beginning of the run—a distance in a straight line of about a hundred miles.

The story in these bald outlines was known to so many old people among us that my interest was excited, and I set to work to discover the value of the tradition. A letter which I put into the *Field* newspaper began to bring me information from one or two extra-parochial sources. The local version also stated that the hound was picked up and kept alive by a man named Leaney, who was afterwards paid for his trouble by some nobleman to whom the hound belonged. I found a daughter-in-law of this man. She knew it was right, but had forgotten the nobleman's name. A letter from the son of an old M.F.H. in Wiltshire told me that the tradition of this run was well known there, though the locality of its end was forgotten. I was advised to try my informant with the name of Lord Castlehaven. Upon receiving this clue I went to my old parishioner, and, after some conversation, asked her whether the nobleman was Lord Castlehaven. She had been perfectly staunch when I had mentioned the names of other noblemen ; but the start she gave when she heard the name Castlehaven, and the unhesitating manner in which she said, " Yes, that was the name," would, I believe, have convinced the veriest sceptic that Lord Castlehaven was, at any rate, the nobleman of the tradition. Putting together, therefore, the fact that the tradition of the fox and hound being found dead of exhaustion, with one more hound all but dead, is known in Wiltshire and in Sussex, and the further fact that in Wiltshire the tradition is coupled with Lord Castlehaven's pack, while in Sussex Lord Castlehaven was the nobleman whom the story assigns as the owner of the hounds, I think we may fairly say that a run beginning somewhere near Grovely House, not far from Wilton, where Lord Castlehaven had his kennels, ended in a field near our village. The spot where the fox and hounds were discovered was shown to an old man now alive by the person who found them, and the daughter-in-law of the man who kept the surviving hound till it was claimed, and who got paid

for keeping it, was my informant on the point of the
name of the nobleman, so that the evidence seems
reasonably conclusive. Anyone who takes a map
and measures even the shortest distance between
Wilton, near Salisbury, and a point almost equally
distant from Tunbridge Wells and Hastings, and in a
straight line between the two towns, will see the
remarkable nature of the run. I have in vain
searched the *Gentleman's Magazine*, in which publication a correspondent tells me that he remembers
having seen a notice of the run, and I should be
thankful if anyone could refer me to the exact volume.
The date of the transaction must have been, as nearly
as I can make out, some year towards the beginning
of this (nineteenth) century or the end of the last,
though it is true that the paragraph in the magazine
may have been a reference to the matter in after-time,
and not a contemporary account.

I cannot, however, discover that even in our very
roughest times we ever reached in this part of East
Sussex the roughness which characterized the sports
popular in my native parish in Cheshire almost within
my own lifetime. It was only about the year 1824
that public bear-baiting at the wakes and on the
Wakes Sunday, as I always understood, was put a
stop to. A worthy woman, on whose word I could
implicitly rely, has told me that when she was a
child her little brother and herself took it into their
heads to buy half a pound of treacle and smear it
over a number of posts, placed to keep carts out of the
ditch, in the lanes along which the bear had to pass
on its way to Bunbury Wakes. She did so, and with
her brother " lay up " to see the results. In due
course the bear appeared, and soon discovered the

sweet stuff, which, as was expected, it proceeded
leisurely to lick. In vain did the " bear-ward " try
to get the animal past the posts, and after sundry
useless attempts he was obliged to take the creature
into a shed close by, where the girl and her brother
were lying hidden, and unmuzzle it, and so let it lick
the more quickly. The poor woman said that the
man's threats of vengeance, which she distinctly
heard him uttering against the authors of the practical
joke, if only he could find them, were so terrible that
neither she nor her brother dared ever say a word
about the matter till they were " man and woman
grown." I understood her also to say that she had
herself seen men fighting, cock-fighting, bear-baiting,
badger-baiting, and horse-racing, all going on at one
time at the wakes. Fighting, indeed, was so completely a part of the business looked forward to at
the wakes, that fights were frequently put off for a
time with the understanding, " I wunna foight thee
now ; I'll foight thee Bunbury Wakes." An old inhabitant of the parish has told me that he well
remembered seeing four or five free fights in progress
on the Wake Sunday within a very short distance
of the parish church, and a large sandpit on the
glebe, now enclosed, was especially devoted to these
combats. On a visit to the parish three or four years
ago, as I was walking along a lane under a high
hedge, I heard a man in an adjoining field talking to
a fellow-workman, who was on the top of a load of
clover hay, about a very notorious fighting man of
fifty years before, in whose transportation, after a
long career of evil-doing, my father, as a magistrate,
had the satisfaction of being instrumental. I own
that, as the familiar name of bygone days caught my

ear, I stopped to listen, and I was rewarded by hearing a perfectly independent version of the American story of the 'Coon and Colonel Scott. It took the form of an exclamation of some stranger, who, being just on the point of beginning a fight with an unknown antagonist, discovered his terrible opponent's name, and immediately said—

" Art thou ' Joemug ' ? Then I give up, for nobody never licked 'Joemug' yet."

This fame of fifty years' duration must have been powerfully earned.

In connection with fighting, a friend, in speaking of his young days, has told me that, having his home in Cheshire, he went to school in the South, and that on one of his journeys, the coach being nearly a day late, it stopped one Sunday morning on a heath at no great distance from London, to let the passengers get out and watch a prize-fight. It seems hard nowadays to realize the fact that such an occurrence took place in the experience of anyone still living. I will not venture to say that a prize-fight has lost its fascination even for our more civilized generation, for I never can forget the wild excitement caused in my own parish by the rumour that a fight was going on at Etchingham between Tom Sayers and Bob Brettle, and the way in which some of my most staid parishioners instantly saddled their horses and galloped off to the scene of action. Still this was a spectacle provided by celebrated professional gladiators ; and our own local sports, even at fairs and feasts, are rapidly ceasing to be discredited by violence and brutality.

IX

CRICKET is, of course, our favourite summer game, though it rarely flourishes in any parish in which there is not some resident gentleman who, being himself fond of it, gives it his personal encouragement. It would seem that in times past our county produced players who were as giants to their degenerate successors. At one of our village matches I remember happening to say that the man then batting was having a good innings. This harmless remark was at once rebuked by a reference to days gone by.

" Ah, well ! " said an old man, " it isn't nothin' to an innings I mind a man havin' at ' The Wells ' [Tunbridge Wells] time as I used to go carrier to ' The Borough '—he was in three days, he was, and never was out."

I signified my admiration.

" Yes," added the man, " I know it was three days, for I mind he was in when I went by with the broad wheel wagon to London, and he was in when I came back."

It was a single-wicket match, it is true—so the man said ; still, my recollections pale before his. This statement has been verified to me. The match was between Mr. Thomas Foster, of Penshurst, and Mr. W. Richardson, of Leigh, on the one side, and two well-known players, Messrs. Cooper and Driver, on the other. It was played on Southborough Common, near Tunbridge Wells, in some year between 1816 and 1820. A nephew of Mr. Foster, the hero of the three days' innings, has kindly sent me this corroboration of the remark which I casually heard on our cricket-ground.

Country cricket matches are not bad schools for studying country human nature, and they would furnish matter for " large discourse " to anyone who had fairly wide opportunities of attending them. The following account, as I heard it some years since, came, I believe, from the neighbourhood of Eton or Windsor. A rustic match was just beginning, when it was discovered that an umpire was wanting. After some delay the only man who could be prevailed upon at all to act was a " bargee," and he would not undertake the office till he had let it be clearly understood that he knew little about the game. However, being entreated to stand, and to do his best, he consented. After a series of more or less remarkable decisions, he gave a man " out " on grounds so palpably wrong that the man refused to go out. The players crowded round the umpire, and there was a general commotion. The " bargee " stood perfectly unmoved, with his thumbs in the arm-holes of his waistcoat ; and at length, when he thought that the noise had lasted long enough, he said with a stentorian voice—

" Well, gentlemen, hi'm humpire, and hin or hout, out 'ee goes."

I trust that English respect for lawfully constituted authority at once recognized the reasonableness of the ruling, and that the game went on.

I well remember the first introduction of cricket into the parish of Cheshire in which I was born, and the astonishment of a well-known local quoit-player who begged leave to bowl a few balls to the two Winchester boys who were in. He took a deliberate aim as with a quoit, and then pitched up a ball, which, but for the intervention of the batsman, would undoubtedly have taken the middle stump ; as it was, ball after ball was hit away with a certainty and a vigour which sorely puzzled him, and he was obliged to own that there was some secret in bowling which his skill in quoits did not serve to reveal.

One of our principal indoor resources is music, and though the standard which we reach is not very high, the enjoyment obtained from music in our parish is, I believe, very considerable. There was, I fear, more enthusiasm for the art in a past generation, if the labour and time necessary to reach any fair degree of proficiency in various instruments was a test. Fifty years ago there were many more instrumentalists among us than there are now, though there was, I imagine, less vocal music. We had in those older days frequent gatherings for practice, and if anybody now were to accompany me some winter's evening along the paths by which Mr. Gibson, a farmer of Glazier's Forge, used to send up his bass viol strapped on to a labourer's back, a distance of nearly three miles, he would, I am sure, confess the power of music to charm the Sussex breast.

Our choirmaster and general music director was a worthy man of the name of Fleming, who was also our hairdresser and wigmaker. He had mastered the ordinary rules of music composition, and left behind him sundry hymn-tunes and anthems written in the rural ecclesiastical style then in fashion. His three daughters were our leading church singers, and have it on the authority of his son that one Sunday between the services his father " knocked together " a hymn-tune, which was performed in the afternoon service of that day. We are told that the overture to " Don Giovanni " was written after the general rehearsal the night before the first representation of the opera, and that it was played, without rehearsal, from copies the ink of which was little more than dry ; but then our village *capel-meister* was not Mozart, nor his tune a composition by the author of " Don Juan " ; still, be the tune what it might, the feat was one which is not, I imagine, often attempted or accomplished. His son succeeded him in his business and in his office as choir-master. A man more honestly fond of music, more versatile as a performer, or more ingenious as a constructor and repairer of musical instruments in general, could, I am sure, but rarely be found. The good man built an organ for our church, and the contrivances connected with its mechanism were many and marvellous. He played it himself, but when he died he left no one possessed of the secret of managing the instrument, so it had to make way for another built on more conventional principles. He was my organist till he died, and I do not recollect that we ever fell out on the subject of music, or on any other subject either, during all the years we knew each other. He had a kindly word for every one, and he had in return the good will, I believe, of all his fellow-parishioners. Before the more common use of pianofortes, the presence of himself and his fiddle was essential at any parochial gathering where a dance was an element of the programme, and so completely had country dances become, as it were, part of himself, that it is currently reported that he used to keep on playing long after he had fallen asleep through weariness or fatigue. Music was in the family, and I remember once calling upon one of his sisters who had long been suffering severe pain with rheumatism, but who on that particular occasion told me that she had been lying on the sofa a great part of the afternoon, thinking, in spite of her pain, " what a heavenly mind that man Handel must have had when he wrote the ' Hallelujah Chorus.' "

The special power of this wonderful chorus in raising the hearer's thoughts above this material world I have heard curiously exemplified in the case of a listener who was hearing the " Messiah " for the first time. She was apparently the wife of a tradesman, and her conversation about music before the oratorio began had interested me considerably. After the " Hallelujah Chorus " was finished—and it had been remarkably well sung—I turned round to my friend, partly out of curiosity, to see what impression it had made. She immediately said to me, with a kind of awe—

" Ah, sir ! what will this be in another world ! "

The same sentiment I have heard attributed to my late good friend Dr. Stephen Elvey, the organist of New College, Oxford, whose love of Handel's music was equalled only by his power of interpreting that music to others. After the performance of the chorus at the ceremony of the opening of the Crystal Palace at Sydenham, I was told that he was heard to say—

" What will this be in heaven ! "

One more criticism of this marvellous chorus I may mention. We had sung it with about fifty voices at an East Sussex village concert, which I was conducting. The orchestra was very crowded, and the room was very full and very hot. We had sung " lustily,

and with good courage," and the audience had enthusi-
astically, though somewhat unmercifully, encored the
chorus. We repeated it, and at the end of the repeti-
tion, when our ideas of the greatness of the music and
its theme were, or ought to have been, at their highest,
I heard one of the singers say earnestly, as he passed
his hand over his forehead—

" Well, that's a sweater ! "

One item of the programme at the same concert was
" Angels ever Bright and Fair," which was sung with
a purity of style and a depth of feeling not yet forgotten by some who heard it. When the singer had
finished, I overheard one of the choir-boys whisper to
his neighbour—

" I say, Tom, I like that better than buttered
beans ! "

The full meaning of this criticism we can only
appraise by comparing it with the utterance of an
alderman who should say that he preferred a sym-
phony of Beethoven to a Mansion House dinner !
Buttered beans I took to be the highest form of pleasure
the boy had hitherto known.

Some years ago, having an hour to spare after
attending a meeting at Brighton, I strolled into the
Pavilion grounds, where a flower show was being
held, and listened to the band of the Coldstreams.
One of the pieces was a bassoon solo, which was played
with great ability, and with apparently a keen perception of the capacity of the instrument for producing
grotesque sounds. At some point of the performance
in which the rapid transitions from deep bass to falsetto
especially amused me, I smiled, whereupon a man
standing near me, who probably had never heard a
solo on the bassoon before, and who evidently had

long had his doubts as to the *bonâ fide* nature of the exhibition, came close to me and said, very confidentially—

" D'you think he's tight, sir ? "

I have heard the Coldstreams once or twice since, and each time I have felt sorely tempted to tell the clever bassoon-player what effect his skill on that particular occasion had on a Sussex auditor.

A sympathetic audience is of the highest importance to a performer, and had the bassoon-player known how his efforts were being received, his artistic enthusiasm would, I fear, have been more damped than whetted. I have myself experienced the effects of want of appreciation. After the taking of Sebastopol in 1855 I was, I remember, singing, at a parochial gathering at the vicarage of the parish in which I was then curate, a patriotic song, entitled " Sebastopol is Won." However imperfect the performance might have been, it certainly did not lack the quality of vigour, and my heart, at any rate, was with the music. When I finished there was a dead silence, an ominous silence, which was, however, shortly broken by an inquiry addressed by one of my audience in a distinct voice to a brother farmer—

" Sold your pony yet ? "

My thoughts were at once recalled from the bloodstained slopes of the Malakoff and the Redan ; the conversation speedily took an agricultural turn, and in less than two minutes Sebastopol and the song were alike forgotten. The war, however, had certainly stirred the patriotism of such of my parishioners as frequented the " King's Arms," a popular hostelry, unfortunately almost exactly opposite my house. The form which the parochial excitement took was chiefly a condemnable iteration of " Red, White, and Blue," sung on the strength of much cider, with a rude energy which, about eleven o'clock on Saturday nights, was surprising and almost painful. One Saturday night, however, the house was almost quiet, and for a fortnight I heard scarcely a sound of the familiar song. Being somewhat puzzled to account for the change, I inquired of a regular frequenter of the house what had happened. He replied at once—

" Why, there, sir ; the man as used to make such a row, sir, he burst a blood-vessel, quavering on his high G."

I found that it was a fact that the man had lost his voice, though, not like Falstaff, by " holloaing and singing of anthems," yet by the bursting of a blood-vessel consequent on his patriotic exertions in leading " Red, White, and Blue," and similar melodies. Nature in this case came to the rescue, and delivered us from the uproar by applying a remedy which I once heard recommended with good results in a coffee-room at Gravesend.

I had walked over with a friend, and we had gone into one of the hotels to get some refreshment and to look out on the river. At a table in a bow-window not far from us was a child, which was incessantly asking its fond father and mother, in a very shrill voice, questions of no more general interest than—

" Where does that ship come from ? " " Where is that ship going ? " and the like.

The annoyance was considerable, though no one seemed exactly to know how to stop it. At last three very gentlemanly-looking young men came in, seated themselves at a table, and gave their orders. They soon found the child's noise insufferable, and one of them, in a very quiet but decided tone, and the most ordinary, business-like manner, called out—

" Waiter."

" Yessir," was the immediate response.

" Choke that child," was the concise instruction given.

I will not say that a second " Yessir " reached my ears, but the effect was instantaneous. The good lady and her child disappeared in a trice, and we were at peace.

Sussex musical criticisms in our local papers have also at times afforded me considerable amusement, mixed with astonishment. The quaint conceits which occasionally are printed are sometimes simply uncorrected mistakes of compositors who cannot decipher the manuscript sent to them ; at other times they are mistakes made consciously by persons who must know that they are going out of their way to show their ignorance. What else can be said of the following criticism of Pinsuti's impassioned part-song, " The Sea hath its Pearls " ?—" The next piece was ' The Sea hath its Perils,' which brought to mind vivid recollections of the Handel Festival." Probably all that the writer meant was to show his readers that he had heard " Israel in Egypt " at the Handel Festival, and that he remembered something about " the horse and his rider being thrown into the sea," but his conscience ought to have pricked him when he wrote that this thought was suggested by Pinsuti's music and " The Sea hath its Pearls."

To any musical reader who knows the " St. Paul," the chorus, " How lovely are the Messengers ! " will be familiar, though he might be fairly pardoned for not recognizing it under the title " How Lonely are

the Passengers ! " attributed to it by the Sussex newspaper critic. But perhaps the perversion to which, in
the elegant Latinity of the same paper, " the appro-
priate motto, ' Palmaur qui ferat muralt,' " may be
applied, is the following description of Stevens' well-
known glee, " The Cloud-capt Towers." " Then
followed a glee, ' The Cloud,' Capt. Towers." Capt.
Towers was printed as the performer's and not the
composer's name, so that the confusion was complete.
It was in a north country, and not a Sussex paper,
that I once read, " Andante—a minor sympathy—
Mendelssohn," as one of the pieces performed at a
concert.

I suppose that in country newspapers paragraphs
are printed off just as they are set up, without intervention of editorial eyes, or these delightful blunders
would not occur, and the papers would be duller than
they are. I was once staying with a friend who, at a
large and enthusiastic meeting the night before, had
made a truly eloquent and able speech, into which he
had boldly introduced a quotation of a couple of lines
of Homer in their original language. The next morning the printer's boy brought the proofs to be cor-
rected, so the world lost one of the most wonderful
specimens of the Greek language ever published. I
was reading aloud the proof, and I had got on fairly
well till I came to the quotation, of which I was obliged
to confess that I could make neither head nor tail.
The characters were Greek, it is true, and there was a
semblance of words, but there all similarity to Greek
ceased. I showed it to my learned host, who at once
rang the bell, and sent for the boy to ask whether he
could give any explanation of the puzzle. His statement was prompt and straightforward—

" Please, sir, we sent to all the printing-offices in town, and those were all the Greek letters we could get."

Had not the speech been an important one, and of sufficient consequence to be sent to its author for revision, the two lines of Homer might have been presented to the public in the original guise in which I saw them, and had they been so, I will venture to say that many copies of the paper would have been bought as a curiosity by members of the learned audience before which the speech was delivered. The lines were forthwith translated and appeared in English. Personally I have no right to complain of the exemption of our country musical reports from editorial supervision, as the most hearty praise that I ever got from a reporter was due to a mistake. A young lady at a concert in which I was taking part had sung a recitative remarkably well, but on reading the account of the performance in our local newspaper, I found to my surprise that this particular recitative had been " splendidly declaimed " by myself.

One of the truest maxims on the subject of musical criticism that I ever heard, was casually enunciated by a German gentleman, sitting in front of me at a concert of the old London Musical Society. I heard him say to his friend—

" Well, in my opinion there are two kinds of people who ought to give their opinions about music ; those who know enough about it to be able to give an opinion which is really valuable, and those who simply say what they like, and what they don't like, and no more."

For my own part I sincerely believe that our natural instincts in matters of art, if honestly followed without being vitiated by that little learning which is a dangerous thing, or by that fear of being thought behind the world and contemptibly provincial which is equally dangerous, are sufficiently healthy to secure us much truer art than that which is supplied to the demand of fashionable opinion and mere cuckoo-criticism.

" Dear lost companions of the tuneful art," sings the poet, but we in our parish may speak not only of the loss of companions in a particular art but of the loss within late years of sundry arts themselves. People who are wont nowadays to look to the large centres of commerce for almost anything they want, may be surprised to know how comparatively independent of outside help many of our country parishes were fifty or sixty years ago. Within the recollection of many persons still alive we grew flax, bleached it, carded it, spun, and wove it at home. In many of our cottages there are yet to be found sheets, table-cloths, and other articles of linen which seem to defy the power of time. Doubtless they are now kept more as curiosities than for use ; still they have borne an amount of wear and tear which is certainly not expected of more modern goods.

We had our own hatter within my own memory, though when I knew him he had ceased to work at his trade. His productions had the character of being everlasting. It was said to be simply impossible to wear them out. One particular kind of hat, called " dog's-hair " hats, had this further peculiarity, that if a man wished to reach something, say from a shelf, and found himself hardly tall enough, he had nothing to do but to put down his hat upon the ground and stand upon it ; it would bear him without a sign of yielding. A man who used to wear one of these imperishable helmets told me that till it had got well sweated to the shape of the head, wearing it was " all one as if you had your head in the stocks." The two finer kinds of material used in our hats were " hare's flick " or " rabbit flick." Hats of the former kind were, I believe, expensive and quite aristocratic, and were reserved principally for Sundays and special occasions.

We had also our hairdresser and wig-maker, who was a superior artist, and who employed several hands exclusively in the wig department. He himself, so his son told me, used to go regularly twice a week to the house of one of his principal customers " to weave his cue," or, in less professional language, to plait his pigtail. He would, I imagine, have scorned the line of business which the village barber in another county must have accepted, if a boy to whom I once spoke on the subject of hair-cutting told the truth. I happened to say to the lad—

" Tommy, why don't you get your hair cut ? You can hardly see out of your eyes."

" Please, sir," said the boy, " I haven't got no money."

" Why," I said, " how much does the barber charge ? "

" A penny, sir, and twopence if he don't nock it [notch it]," was the reply.

I have often regretted that I did not give the boy a penny, and tell him to go at once and get the cheaper tonsure, and then come back and show me the result. Had the snipping been too outrageously haphazard, I could but have sent him with another penny to have the notches obliterated, and I should have been really curious to see what was considered a fair pennyworth of haircutting.

Whether in town or country, the conventional conversation of hairdressers is frequently not of a high order, and I question whether the following anecdote, of which a near relation of my own was the victim, is often equalled in originality. The hairdresser began with probably a well-accustomed opening—

" A fine head of hair, sir, for a gentleman of your time of life, sir ! "

The gentleman, who was not in the habit of talking much on such occasions, signified that he heard the remark, but said nothing. The hairdresser proceeded.

" Very odd, sir, but I never knew clever men have much hair, sir."

Another grunt, but nothing more, whereupon the cruel climax followed.

" It's a very singular thing, sir, but I never met with a bald idiot in all the course of my practice ! "

Why a bald man, idiot or not, should go to a hair-cutter did not appear, but this by the way. Whether the series of remarks was meant as a punishment for the non-appreciation of the compliment conveyed in the first was never known.

I was once myself completely deceived by what I can imagine to be a common joke in the trade, but for which I was not prepared at the moment. I asked whether " the principal," who usually " waited upon me," was disengaged. The assistant replied in, as I thought, a very serious tone.

" He's upstairs, sir ; he's dying, sir."

" Dear me ! " I replied ; " I am very sorry to hear it. Has he been ill long ? "

" He's dyeing a gentleman's hair, sir ; he will be

at liberty in a few minutes," was the reassuring answer.

Though I was of course glad that my worst fears had not been realized, I was still conscious of having been unwarily sympathetic.

Many years ago the master of one of the London Companies told me that he had invited his hairdresser to a livery dinner of the Company, and that on going to the shop the next time he asked him how he liked the entertainment.

" Oh, sir, splendid, sir—splendid ! "

" Did you like the turtle-soup ? "

" Oh, sir, first class ! "

" How often were you helped ? "

" Only once, sir."

" Only once, my good friend ?   Why did you throw away a chance like that ? "

" Oh, sir, I had been told that it was not genteel to soup twice," was the poor man's expression of bitter regret.

But from wig-makers to wigs. I have been told of a man who emigrated from Sussex to America falling out with his landlady, and in his wrath throwing a stool at her head and carrying away her wig. Not knowing that she wore a wig, and thinking that the blow had scalped her, he is reported to have rushed out of the house, and having sent for his things, to have returned as speedily as possible to his native land. Wig-making, however, and its kindred arts have now been carried elsewhere, and in this respect we have retrograded. Many of our smaller villages have, no doubt, at all times been very dependent upon foreign help in matters even of the first necessity, and I quite remember a clergyman, a new-comer into the diocese, being congratulated on the progress of his

MASTER RAGUE KEMP WEARING SUSSEX "ROUND-FROCK," 1923

parish—it having been rumoured that now " a tailor called on Tuesdays."

Our great local industry of the past age was, of course, iron. It is a well-known story that the iron railings which till lately surrounded St. Paul's Cathedral were the product of a forge in, I believe, that part of Lamberhurst parish which is in Sussex, and an old man used to tell me that he remembered the last forge in this district—I believe at Ashburnham —ceasing to work. Among lesser local industries, besides weaving, spinning, and " wig-making," that have died out within the memory of man, we may include the making of those " round frocks," which were the pride and glory of an East Sussex labourer fifty years ago. Never more shall we see " Tom Cladpole " start for London, arrayed in one of these frocks ; in leather leggings, the special production of native talent ; in a hat made in his own parish ; in half-boots which could have been made nowhere else ; and with an umbrella which, if not made at home, had been made after a strictly home pattern. For better or worse, these things are gone past recall. Coming through our parish soon after the time of which I am speaking, our friend might have stopped to eat his " brencheese " at the " Labour-in-Vain," under a sign painted by a native artist, Master Upfield, who lived near " Heffle " Church, representing a blackamoor in a tub, with two men trying to scrub him white. Now he would stop at the " Railway Tavern," where the accommodation would be all that he could require, but, alas ! the humour of the sign would be gone. In short, the change produced by the last fifty years in Master Cladpole's outward appearance, in his manner of speech, in his methods of locomotion, and, in some respects, in the man himself, has been so complete that it is even now difficult to realize it. He probably started in life fully impressed with the wisdom of the advice which a Sussex man has told me that he used to receive, almost word for word, from one of his seniors—advice the serious nature of which is well represented by the wondrous series of negatives in which it was conveyed—

" Mind," the old man would say to his young friend, " mind you don't never have nothing in no way to do with none of their new-fangled schemes."

This astonishing formula of Conservative prudence finds its match in negatives, it is true, in the half-indignant inquiry which I have heard attributed to a huntsman on our Downs, who, the fox having run to earth, exclaimed with ungrammatical energy—

" What ! hasn't nobody got *never* a terrier as can't show us nothin' where the old fox has gone ? "

But neither wisdom nor indignation can struggle long against Her Majesty's Inspectors of Schools in the matter of grammar, and if they would still secure a hearing they must conform to more modern modes of expression. Tom Cladpole's children and the old huntsman's children already smile at their parents' Sussex speech. They know that two negatives make an affirmative, and I only hope that in other things also they are equally wiser than their fathers. Their thoughts, moreover, in general are more set on the present and the future than on the past, and in a few years more the means of reproducing the past will be less still than they are even now.

In a few more years it will surely not be possible to hear again in a Sussex school the following col-loquy :—

Master (on his rounds)—" Tommy, you dirty little boy, blow your nose ! "

Master (on returning in about a quarter of an hour)—" Tommy, you dirty little boy, why didn't you blow your nose when I told you ? "

Tommy (unabashed)—" Please, sir, I did blow 'er, but 'er wouldn't bide blowed."

I fancy that already an answer which I got some years ago from a small boy at Burwash Weald must belong to a bygone purely voluntary system—

I—" You ought to be at school, my little man."

He—" Gooin' this afternoon, verlike."

If I live to meet in ten years' time a parishioner on the road with a bag of something on his " wheels," he will hardly tell me that he has " been to get a poke of chaff to help to make up his bed with." The " wheels " will probably be a pony-cart, and the " poke of chaff " a bag of goose-feathers, or a spring mattress.

If he has got a job of woodcutting in " the top cant of Rolf's Gill," he will most likely explain its whereabouts in less old-fashioned monosyllables than these ; and if, later on in the year, he gets crushed with a " timber-tug " in clearing the wood for the timber merchant, he possibly may not have the nerve, as one of my present parishioners had, to bring his great toe-nail home in his waistcoat pocket.

" Contrairiness " and contradiction we shall certainly have as long as our parish exists ; but will our " contrairy " ones mingle humour with their contradictions, as did one of their forefathers ?

He was coming out of the " Rose and Crown " late at night many years ago, and by way of a natural answer to his companion, who happened to remark how dark it was, retorted at once—

" No, it ain't dark—it ain't a bit dark—it ain't dark at all."

He had not gone above twenty yards when he ran full face into the sign-post which stands in the street at the end of the lane. The shock, however, far from drawing forth any confession of error, simply produced the exclamation—

" Dear me, how fast it has come on dark ! "

Untruthful parishioners we shall, alas ! also have ; but will they be as ingenious in their falsehoods as another of their ancestors, whose reputation as a most " onaccountable " liar is largely based on an often-repeated asseveration, " that in one place he'd bin to, the rainbows were t'other side uppards ? "

Benefit Clubs may continue, but will they ever have again such a feast-day as a west-country club was described to me as having had some years ago ?—

" Oh ! ma'am, the procession were beautiful, and at the end of it, all the widows that were upon the club came along riding in a wagon, and the club stewards had made up a grave in the wagon, and had covered it with turf, and all the widows sat round it, makin' believe to weep, and they used their handkerchers as naytral as naytral."

Eclipses will still be described in the almanacks as " partial " ; but will the rustics of the future express their surprise that an eclipse should be seen in London as well as in the country, by the remark which a countryman not long ago made to a friend of mine who had stated that he too had seen the eclipse " in town " ?

" Oh, then, sir, 'twur pretty general."

Doubtless hereafter " Sussex folk " will be superior to their grandfathers in knowledge and exact science

—they will possibly also earn more money—and they will live better. I pray that they may be happier also, and that together with better times, honesty and good faith between man and man may also increase and abound and that such honourable doctrines as a fair day's work for a fair day's wage, as well as a fair day's wage for a fair day's work, may not perish with all the picturesqueness of our Sussex life in the olden times.

I have now gathered together such of my " recollections " of humble life—for they have rarely passed beyond that sphere—as seem to me to illustrate the country human nature, and particularly the Sussex country human nature, in which I have long taken a heartfelt interest. What I have written I believe to be, at any rate, genuine. Dignity, I fear, it has none ; and that it has not more humour, more pathos, and more serious reality, is the fault, alas ! of my imperfect perception, and certainly not of human nature.

LECTURE ON THE HISTORY OF THE PARISH OF BURWASH[1]

Delivered in the National Schoolroom, Burwash, on Monday, March 6, 1871, and Monday, March 6, 1876.

BEFORE I begin my lecture I must acknowledge my obligations to the interesting article on Burwash, by Mr. C. F. Trower, in the twenty-first volume of the " Sussex Archæological Collections," and also to Mr. Durrant Cooper for historical suggestions which greatly assisted me in my compilation. But for these helps I do not know that I should have made the present humble attempt to follow in their steps.

It was, I believe, Defoe who said that people who boast of their ancestors are like potatoes, in that " their best part is underground."

Boasting, however, apart, we instinctively feel an interest in any scrap of history which connects our family, or our country, or our parish, with the past, especially if that past be in any way one of credit ; and from this feeling, at any rate on my own part, this lecture springs.

First, then, as to our name—what is it ? And here, then,

---

[1] *This lecture was not finally revised by the author, but it contains so much interesting information respecting the past life of Burwash that it seemed to deserve preservation. The Editor has compared it very carefully with the author's MS., and has rarely ventured on any verbal alteration. Stories contained in the previous pages have been generally omitted, but it is hoped that two or three repetitions may be excused, as they could not be avoided without marring the connection of thought.—H. W.*

I may confess at once it is hard to say. There are at least fifteen different ways of spelling it ; and Burwese, Burwash, Burgwash, Borwershe, Burghersh, Burghurst, are a few of the variations out of which you may take your choice. That the name is Saxon is clear.

Secondly, as to its meaning. The local tradition on this point respecting the dog " Bur " need not be repeated to you.[1] But a little time since I appealed to an old college tutor of mine, formerly professor of Anglo-Saxon in the University of Oxford, to know whether he could give me any other derivation of the name Burwash, Burghersh, or Burghurst, and he kindly sent me three possible ones. Burghurst, " the wood on the hill," or, quære, " the hill of the wood " ; Burgherse, or Burghersh, " high hill pastures or fields "—so Won-ersh in Surrey—and Burwœse, " a swamp or miry place on the hill," or, quære, " a hill in a swamp." Now, seeing how Burwash on the east, north, and south sides rises as it were out of flats which are now often flooded, and which, a thousand years ago, were probably little better than marshes or swamps, I am not at all sure that " wœse," the Saxon word for marsh, swamp, morass, may not be the original form of the termination " wash," and Burwœse or Burwash might then mean the hill in the morass. Burewese is the spelling in 1246.

And now to our history. Though Mr. Trower in his

[1] See p. 58 of this volume. " Even though there be no truth in the legend, yet certainly it is a legend worth commemorating."— Dean Stanley, Wednesday, June 12, 1872, at a dinner in the Hall of University College, Oxford, on the celebration of the thousandth anniversary of the (legendary) foundation of the college by King Alfred.

The only being of the name of " Bur " that I have ever heard of is a man of whom it is written in the old Icelandic legends (Edda Sæmundi, Edda Snorri, ed. Thorpe, London : Trübner, 1866 quoted by M. Taine in his " History of English Literature," vol. i p. 33, ed. Edmonston and Douglas, Edinburgh, 1871): " Then the cow Andhumbla, born also of melting snow, brings to light, while licking the hoar-frost from the rocks, a man ' Bur,' whose grandsons kill the great Ymir."

There was some years ago a man of the name of Burr, with two r's, on Burwash Common.

article very fairly, I think, argues, from a document of
22 Edw. I (1294), that the manor of Burwash was in
existence possibly within ten years of the date of the
Domesday Book (say 1096), still the first actual notice of
Burwash, as far as I know, is one to which my attention
was called by Mr. Durrant Cooper, in the Close Rolls of
the 31st of Hen. III, or A.D. 1246—625 years, that is, ago.
On the 28th of August in that year, the king granted to
Guilbert of Kent, to be held by himself and his successors
the parsons of Burwash for ever, land which the Countess
of Eu had given to Robert Faber. Who Robert Faber
was I cannot tell, but fifty years after this time there was
a wealthy family of this name in Mayfield (S. A. C., xxi. 2),
and there may have been some connection between the
two. As there was a parson of Burwash at this date,
there probably was a church ; and part of the tower, at all
events, of our Burwash Church is old enough to have seen
Guilbert of Kent and some of his predecessors, if there
were any. It may interest the owners of Dudwell mill,
and of Mr. Russell's mill, to know that on the same day
on which the grant of land was made to the parson of
Burwash, the king also signed an order to the bailiff of
the manor of Burwash, being bailiff of the lands [1] which
had belonged to the Countess of Eu, to build a mill on the
manor, which mill we may almost certainly say stood
where one or other of the two mills now stands. Mr.
Trower gives a copy of the particular account of the manor
of Burwash in the year 1280, and there we find the rent
of a water-mill set at one mark, or 13s. 4d. per annum,
and it seems assumed on all hands that the Park Farm

[1] S.A.C., vii. 49. The Eu property was confiscated 29 Hen. III,
A.D. 1244 ; and in Knight's " Popular History of England " I find
the following statement (i. 368). In 1244 the King of France said in
a declaration, " As it is impossible that any man living in my kingdom, and having possessions in England, can consistently serve two
masters, he must either inseparably attach himself to me or to the
King of England." Henry went further, and ordered that the
French in England, especially the Normans, should be dispossessed
without a choice.

is the site of the park of the Lords of Burwash manor, so that a mill on that manor would, as I have said, almost certainly be where either Dudwell mill or Mr. Russell's mill now is. The account of the manor is in these days interesting, as a means of comparison between our own Burwash and the Burwash of six hundred years ago. " There is a capital (or chief) mansion, which is worth annually, in herbage, garden produce, and a certain area in front of the gate, 7s. 6d." By way of explanation of such a sum as this, we may say that the best authorities on the value of money in those times tell us that the money of that day, taking silver at 5s. an ounce, may be valued at three times the same denomination in the present day (Jacob on Precious Metals, i. 322, quoted in Knight's " Popular History of England," i. 366) ; and Mr. Hallam (Knight's " Popular History," i. 396) considers any given sum under Henry III and Edward I as equivalent in general command over commodities to about twenty-four or twenty-five times its nominal value at present—that is, that a shilling six hundred years ago would buy as much as 24s. or 25s. would buy now. In those reigns the average price of wheat was 6d. a bushel ; a sheep might be bought for 1s., an ox for 10s. But to go on with par-ticulars of Burwash Manor—" eighty-seven acres of arable land in the demesne (as well within as outside the park) which are worth annually £1 1s. 9d. ; the price of an acre is 3d." I find that in A.D. 1288, in Suffolk, in the parish of Hawstead, the highest rent was 7d. an acre, and some land was let as low as a farthing an acre (see Knight, i. 398) ; and in 1390, in the same parish, the average yield of wheat was six bushels per acre. Burwash farming could not, I should think, have been very much behind Suffolk then, whatever it is now. The sale of the underwood in the park was worth, per annum, 9s. ; the sale of the heather, 12d. ; warren and conies, or rabbits, 4s. ; and the water-mill, one mark. The toll of wagons passing through the forest, 12d. The freeholders pay

41s. 1½d. a year. One bow and four arrows, worth 4d.; one pound of pepper, worth 10d. (within 2d. the value of the toll of all the wagons for twelve months); one pair of gilt spurs, 6d.; three hens and a cock, 5½d.; half a pound of cummin worth one-eighth of a penny. The whole worth £18 2s. 1½d.

In 1294 (22 Edw. II) John, Duke of Brittany, grants and confirms to the treasury of the Free Chapel in the Castle of Hastings, the tenth penny of his demesne lands, to be paid yearly by his sheriffe, viz. of Burghershe, 12d. (S. A. C., xiii.); and, in 1306, our parish makes its first step, if we may say so, on to the stage of our national history, for in that year died Robert de Burghersh, its owner, who took his name from the property. This Robert was a man of note, a member of Parliament, Constable of Dover, and Warden of the Cinque Ports, an office held by the late Duke of Wellington, and now by Lord Granville; so that our name now had got beyond our woods, and was heard in courts and camps.

A son of this Robert de Burghersh, or, as some say, a grandson, was Bishop of Lincoln, twice Lord Treasurer, and once Lord Chancellor of the kingdom. His father, or, according to the other genealogy, his brother Stephen, owner of the manor, obtained, as soon as he came to the property, a grant from the crown of free warren, or right of hunting beasts of prey and chase in the demesne lands of the manor. I had in my hand the other night the actual parchment on which was written a grant of just this date by the king, of free warren to Robert de Passelye over the manor of Pashley and other properties. It is in the possession of Mr. Nathan Wetherell, the present owner of Pashley, and is a curious link between ourselves and times so long gone by. In our Burwash woods then very possibly young Henry de Burghersh, more than five hundred and fifty years ago, contracted the love of sport, which did not desert him even when he was a bishop. Must we say it? Henry de Burghersh, Bishop of Lincoln, kept hounds—a sad instance, by-the-by, as I once heard another very reverend divine (Dr. Mansel, Dean of St. Paul's) remark, of clerical dog-matism—and, having hawks and hounds, the bishop must needs make a park on his episcopal manor that he might use them ; and, in order to make a park, he ejected his poorer tenants from their lands, caring little for the curses which most men, not to say most bishops, would have considered no little discount from their sport.[1] The hunting bishop, however, apart from sport, was not in other respects, by all accounts, a man for Burwash or anywhere else to be proud of. Fuller the antiquary says of him, that when we have allowed that he was of noble birth, we have said " all that is to be said in his commendation, he being otherwise neither good for Church nor State, sovereign nor subjects ; covetous, rebellious, ambitious, injurious." Sport seems in that age to have been a great weakness of the clergy, for we find the great Bishop William of Wykeham (my kinsman, I may add, by whose liberality my father and two of my brothers have had their education for almost nothing) very indignant (in 1373) with some canons whom he found to be professed hunters and sportsmen, absolutely forbidding them to " keep hounds by themselves or by others, openly or by stealth, within the convent or without." William of Wykeham was once, we are told, Canon of Hastings (S. A. C., xiii.), and has a shield with his arms in Brightling Church. He therefore may have known something about the Bishop of Lincoln's early and later life too. Before we leave mention of Lincoln, I may add that Mr. Trower says that the singing boys of Lincoln Cathedral are still maintained by the funds of a Burghersh, and that an old house there is still called by the family name. In the matter of sport, Sussex clergy seem to have been great offenders, for in 1524, much later on, and when people ought to have known better, the

---

[1] See at p. 42 the story of the bishop's penance in purgatory for this offence.

prior of Hardham Priory, in West Sussex, was accused before the bishop, not only of sporting, but actually of night-poaching; and his defence was that he did not poach himself, though he owned that he and two more were watching at Bignor Park gate while two men whom he had hired were inside killing the deer, and when the keeper, Master Bager, suddenly came up, he and his men bolted as fast as they could, and left the real poachers in the keepers' hands. Still this was all bad for monks.

In the year 1310 (3rd of Edw. II) John, Duke of Brittany, obtained from the king the grant of a weekly market and of a fair twice a year in the manor of Burwash, so that our fair carts, little as we like them now, may possibly plead a very ancient ancestry of five hundred and sixty years. This market and fair would seem to point out Burwash in those days to have been a place of some importance, though how the farmers got their goods to market every week five or six hundred years ago I hardly know, seeing that there is a man now alive in Burwash, Mr. John Vigor, who tells me that he remembers six horses to a two-wheel cart from Dudwell mill, with the slub up to the cart-axles; and he says that even in the month of May, when his father used to send meat up to Rose Hill, a man would go beside the horse to take the basket off at the worst places, just below Court Barn, while the man or boy on the horse gave all his mind to getting himself and his beast through the mire. The roads hereabouts were not very well suited for light carts, even in Mr. Vigor's early days, seeing that when he was a boy, calves were carried by tying their legs together, and by swinging the poor brutes over a horse's shoulders; while, instead of farmers' wives trusting themselves to gigs, four-wheels, dog-carts, or pony-traps, they used in his boyhood to mount a pillion, and ride on horseback behind their husbands. Mrs. Blundell of Franchise Farm, and Mrs. Langridge of Rye Green Farm, were the last whom he remembers doing this; and if this was seventy years ago, we may imagine that

moving about was no easy matter in Burwash in the days
of Edward II, and yet in 1412 we find (S. A. C., xiii. 158)
Bishop Reade, in making a visitation of this diocese,
travelling from Warbleton to Salehurst in one day—a very
reasonable distance for a cross country day's journey
in Sussex at that date. About this time,[1] 20 Edw. III
(1347), Woodknowle, or Wokenolle, creeps into notice, a
record being in existence of a conveyance by which Johannes
de Cressyngham, Vicar of Burwash, grants to Walter Wokenolle and Joanna his wife, for life, a house, mill, two hundred
acres of arable, three acres of meadow, and sixty of wood,
and rents to the amount of sixty shillings, with their appur-
tenances at Burwash, and after their decease to William
Lonnesford and Joanna his wife (daughter of the said
Walter and Joan), and the heirs of their bodies. In a
subsidy to King Henry IV, levied in 1412, John Lunsford
is assessed as having lands in Burwash worth yearly £20,
and one William Breton is assessed as having lands worth
yearly £30. Who William Breton was, or of whom he held
his property, I do not know ; but the owner of the manor
of Woodknowle held of the manor of Burwash on payment
of a yearly rent of 6d. for a pair of gilt spurs and 10s.

Knowing, as we very often do, only the bare facts of
history, we cannot but be constantly puzzled as to the
circumstances which led to the facts ; and though the
guesses of historians often come in time to pass for history

---

[1] In 14 Edw. III, 1340 (S.A.C., i. 58), Parliament granted the king
a tax of the ninth lamb, the ninth fleece, and the ninth sheaf, and
the return for Burwash is—two carucates of land, of which the ninth
sheaf would be 22s.—(" Carucate "—plough land, as much arable as
could be managed with one plough and the beasts belonging thereto
in a year ; having meadow, pasture, and houses for the householder
and cattle belonging to it. Sir H. Ellis, on Domesday Book, p. 21)—
a holding belonging to the Duke of Brittany and Earl of Richmond
worth 16s. 8d. Land imparked in the park of Burghersh was worth
for the ninth sheaf 12s.
The hide is generally supposed to be equal to a hundred and
twenty acres. In 1086, i.e. the year of Domesday Book, money is
generally estimated at thirty times its present value.—Sir H. James'
Introduction to Domesday Book of Sussex.

itself, still we have very little means of really satisfying our curiosity. We may well wonder what communication there could have been in those days between Burwash and Norfolk, and yet in the year 1343 we find Richard Swafham, parson of Burwash, exchanging his living with John Strongman, parson of Brunsted, near Norwich. To judge by his name, Richard Swafham was a Norfolk man, Swaffham being a town in that county, and so he might wish to get back to his own county; but all this is, of course, mere guesswork, and Richard Swafham may have had no more to do with Swaffham in Norfolk than I have to do with the parish of Egerton in Kent. Still he did exchange, and I may remark by the way that one of my brothers, of whom I spoke just lately, has newly been presented, as a kinsman of William of Wykeham, to a living in Norfolk, not far from Brunsted, so that a sort of relationship between the parson of Burwash and Norfolk has been established after a lapse of five hundred and twenty-eight years. All this seems a long time ago, and yet, if you choose to go into the north aisle of Burwash Church, you can stoop down and examine a piece of iron which was cast about this time, and which has been thought worthy of being engraved in the Rev. C. Boutell's work on sepulchral monuments, and a piece of which was especially begged from me through a friend by Dr. Percy, the head of the Government metallurgical department, to examine with a view of illustrating the history of iron manufacture in England. It is a slab, having on it, in Longobardic characters, " Orate p(ro) annema Jhone Collin "—" Pray for the soul of Joan Collin." This Collin was probably connected with one of the forges in Burwash, as in 1574 we find notices of divers forges (S. A. C., iii. 343) and furnaces of Collyns, Mayes, and others; and at the same time bonds were taken from Thomas Glide of Burwash, and from George Maye of Burwash, who had a forge called Budgell, at the instance of Ralph Hogge, who claimed a right to the sole exportation of cast-iron ordnance. Nor has the art of iron-working even yet quite perished in Burwash, though the material itself is no longer produced here. The beautiful iron gates in the porch of the church were made by Master Daw, the blacksmith, at Franchise, under the direction of J. W. Tilley, Esq., the then owner of Franchise, who presented them to the church on its restoration in 1856.

Whether Burwash in the fourteenth century was an uncomfortable living or not, I cannot say, but in 1383 another parson of Burwash, Rd. Spenge, exchanged, though this time with a nearer neighbour, one Walter Godlake, an Essex clergyman, parson of Wodeham Mortimer, near Maldon. One feels quite curious to know what was the matter in the parish about this time, as in fifteen years after Parson Spenge's exchange, Parson Stillingflet becomes restless, and exchanges with another, Walter Godlak, parson of Berwick (1398). Eighteen years more, and Parson Hugh Estwell is tired of Burwash, and exchanges with Edward Hoper, Vicar of Clymping, near Arundel. After this we hear no more of exchanging for a time, so we must hope that things took a turn for the better. Not much more, however, than fifty years ago the art of tormenting a parson was not extinct. I have been told of one worthy tithe-payer in this parish about that date who would send up to Dr. Mackenzie with a message that he was going to gather fruit, and that the rector must send down a man to take the tithe. The rector's man would go accordingly; the tithe-payer's man would gather ten gooseberries, give the rector's man one, and say, " Master wasn't going to gather any more fruit that day."

At the beginning of the fifteenth century (S. A. C., xiii. 155) the priors of Holy Trinity at Hastings, owing to their priory being out of repair, had to look out for a new place, and they settled at Warbleton.

Sir John Pelham, the lord of the manor of Burwash, did what he could to encourage them, and in 1413 offered them lands in the parish of Warbleton, and in 1443 (21

BURWASH—VILLAGE STREET, SHOWING RAISED PAVEMENT
BORDERED BY CLIPPED LIMES

Hen. VI.) had licence granted him by the king to give the advowson of an acre of land in Burwash for the support of the chaplain in chantry founded in Warbleton, and to build a proper house. I wonder what Burwash acre of land it was, and who has it now ? There is what they call the " chance " meadow behind the Bear Inn, and I have heard that " chance " is some corruption of " chantry," but this I must leave as I find it.

In 1446 Sir J. Pelham, after some long-standing disputes with the Hoo family, obtained full manorial rights over the manor of Burwash, and in his family the manor remained for three hundred years more, down to the middle of the last century. It is from the records of the lord of the manor that we should be able, perhaps, to fill up some parts of this very dull period of Burwash history ; but as we have no access to these records, we must rest in our ignorance.[1] Here, by the way, I may just remark that in 28 Hen. VI (1450) we find a notice of the manor of Totyngworth along with that of Burwash, and I merely mention this for the chance of Totyngworth having been the origin of the name " The Tot," now given to the property owned by A. Gibbs, Esq.—a property, however, which I find described as " The Tot " in our register as far back as 1665. There is a farm in Heathfield parish called Little Tottenworth. Again, in 35 Hen. VI we find a release of the manor of Burwash by one Andrew Thatcher to John Lewknor and others, and I also mention this merely for the chance of tracing the origin of the name " Thatcher's Barn," now applied to a cottage near Witherenden. The " Thatcher's Arms," too, at Perryman's, was perhaps a more ancient title for a public-house than that of its neighbour the " Fuller's Arms," and it was perhaps hardly well changed for the " Woodman."

[1] The Pelham family has left its mark in Burwash by the " buckle " which is on the font, which sign of the buckle of a belt was given with leave to use it as a crest to John de Pelham at the battle of Poictiers (30 Edw. III, Sept. 19, 1356), as a mark of the honour of the French king John surrendering his sword to him.

Here, however, for a hundred years we must lose sight of Burwash, and leave it to vegetate in peace. All the notice that I can find of it during this time being a valuation of assize rents, whatever they were, during Henry VIII's reign (S. A. C., xiii. 176), amounting to £1 4s. 6d. This is, I own, a small stock of knowledge and information about a parish for a hundred years, and if each hundred years contributed no more, I should have had hard work to pad out a lecture.[1]

In 1558, however, we wake into real life, for in that year the registers began which are now kept in the Parish Chest, and from that time to this we have a tolerably regular account of the Cruttendens, Collinses, Hepdens, and Westons, who have been baptized, married, and buried amongst us. The first baptism which is entered is that of Margaret, daughter of John Dawe ; the second that of a Weston ; the third that of a Cruttenden—all of them names familiar to us in Burwash now. In this year there were five marriages, twenty baptisms, and the great number of thirty-five deaths. The Romish Queen Mary did not die till November 17, 1558, so that these registers are a very short link, but still a link of a few months, between us and the old Roman form of faith ; assuming,

---

[1] Since I wrote this I have discovered a piece of information which may interest Mr. Joseph Noakes, the present tenant of Brooksmarl Farm.

In 1542 (S. A. C., iii. 115) the will of Thomas Donet, of Burwash, was made, in which we find the following items :—

" Item—I give to Rose my wyff the lease of my farm of Brooks-mayle with 8 kine, 2 oxen, and 2 marys [mares] the best that she can chuse. Item—I give to Rose my wyff 2 towyeryngs, and 2 twel-montyngs.

" To Jane my wyff's daughter an heiffer of yerys age.

" To John my son all hys cattell that he hath with me, and a cow, &c.

" To Wylliam my son a cow of 5 yers.

" To Harry Donet my godson a calf "—and so on.

He wills also his horse " Marcocke " and a mare called " Trou-leppe," besides nine other head of stock, and money to buy a " port-wys," or " porteus," that is, a service-book for the Church.—Will dated December 22, 1542.

that is, that under Mary the clergy of Burwash kept the old religion which had been interrupted for a few years under Edward VI. Whether any of our people suffered under the persecutions of Mary we do not know, though in Mayfield four martyrs were burnt in 1556 because they would not give up the Protestant faith, and at Master H. Mapham's, at Brick House, there is a fireback with a man and woman being burnt at the stakes. Possibly the Reformation affected us but little, and in the midst of our woods and wilds it may be that the parson quietly exchanged the Mass-book for the Book of Common Prayer, the Roman vestments for the surplice, and Latin for English. That in ten years' time these changes had taken place we may assume, and we have still remaining the chalice and paten which were employed in the new form of worship. They bear date 1568, but who gave them, or how they were bought, there is no record. However, here they are, and they are a visible and tangible connection with the Burwash of more than three hundred years ago.

Among the burials in 1593 I find the entry, " James Thrushe filius populi, Januarii 28, et filius populi, Januarii 29." [1] The meaning of this term " filius populi " I do not know, and I should be thankful for an explanation of it.

At this date there was living at the " Franchise " a well-to-do family of the name of Maye. The then owner was Sir Thomas Maye, and at the " Franchise " was born about the year 1595 a child destined in his own day to fill no small place in the history of literature, and in our day to satisfy us, the parishioners of Burwash, that we have one belonging to us whose wit and learning enabled him to do in some sense more than any other Englishman has ever done. It is true that I cannot find the baptism of

[1] But see a " Law Dictionary, or the Interpreter of Words and Terms used either in the Common or Statute Laws of Great Britain," by Dr. Cowel ; in the Savoy, 1727 ; *sub voce* " Bastard." " His father is not known by order of law, and therefore he is called Filius Populi."

young Thomas Maye in our register, but I do find the baptisms of brothers and sisters before and after the date of his birth ; and as his father, Sir Thomas Maye, who afterwards went to Mayfield, did not buy Mayfield Abbey till the 6th of May, 1597, as Mr. Durrant Cooper tells us, and probably did not at once go to live there, as his son Edward was baptized in Burwash Church on the 3rd of July in that year, and as his mother therefore would hardly have been able in May or June to go through all the fatigue of moving, and as moreover there is no notice of Thomas Maye's baptism in the Mayfield register, we may fairly conclude that the child born in 1595, more than two years before his father left Burwash, was born in Burwash.

Our connection with May is very interesting, and does us credit. Dr. Johnson,[1] no mean authority in criticism, pronounced him the best Latin poet in England. Mr. Hallam, too, whose verdict, at any rate amongst Englishmen, is deemed worthy of the highest respect, says of him : " But the first Latin poetry which England can vaunt is May's ' Supplement to Lucan ' ; this is not only a very spirited poem, but in many places at least an excellent imitation " (Hallam, " Literature of Europe," iii. 54, ed. 1854). Bravo, Burwash ! and such a good imitation was it that foreign critics published it on their own judgment in good editions of Lucan. Bravo, Burwash, again ! The work so famous was a bold undertaking, seeing that it was nothing less than a Latin continuation of a celebrated poem by a celebrated Latin author. I well remember reading the poem as a boy at Shrewsbury, though at the time I little thought that I was ever going to be so intimately connected with it, as I am by being incumbent of the parish in which the man was born who boldly wrote an additional

[1] In the " Journey to the Western Isles of Scotland," by Dr. Johnson, p. 56, ed. 1775, I also find the following apropos of Latin poetry : " The Latin poetry of ' Deliciæ Poetarum Scotorum ' would have done honour to any nation ; at least, till the publication of May's ' Supplement,' the English had very little to oppose."

book to the poem which I was so painfully studying, and
who wrote it so well that if I had had to read it too, I
should probably not have found out the difference, and
should have had as hard work over the imitation as I had
over the original. All the particulars about Mr. May's
life are to be found in almost any of the biographies, though
owing to his father having afterwards lived at Mayfield,
they say that Thomas was born at Mayfield, and so rob
Burwash of the honour which I hope is now restored to it.
In after years Thomas May was appointed Secretary to the
Parliament, and was by the Parliament commissioned to
write the " History of the Long Parliament," a work of
which Mr. Hallam says, " The Parliament had, however,
a writer who did them honour ; May's ' History of the
Parliament ' is a good model of genuine English : he is
plain, terse, and vigorous ; never slovenly, though with few
remarkable passages, and is in style as well as in substance
a kind of contrast to Clarendon " (" Literature of Europe,"
p. 151). By the order of Parliament May had a public
funeral in Westminster Abbey. A monument was erected
to him near the grave of the great antiquary William
Camden, and as a further proof that he was a man of some
note, he was thought worthy of being dug up again by the
Royalists when they came back into power, and of being
flung into a pit in the ground belonging to St. Margaret's
Church close to the Abbey.

In producing Thomas May, Burwash seems to have
exhausted itself for a time, as we do not again boast any
great celebrity for a good many years.[1] In 1633, however,
Thomas Nevitt, citizen and draper of London, who
had married Obedience, daughter of Robert Cruttenden,
of Burwash—this Obedience aforesaid having been born in
1587—left to this parish in her memory certain gifts to

[1] About this date I find a statement that we, with Chattesfield,
which I take to be Catsfield, were assessed to provide one piece of
armour for public defences, viz. a musquet furnished, though this
was not till 1612 (S. A. C., lxxi. 226). Our name then was not unlike
what it is now, and was spelt Burwashe or Burwasshe.

the poor, and fees to the parson for preaching sermons. The fund in 1633, when it was left, amounted to £2 10s. per annum, charged on certain lands in Romney Marsh. The parson's fees are now given to the poor in the dole on St. Thomas's Day, and the whole amounted in 1857 to £3 6s. 1d., and is now, I think, rather more. Our good friend and benefactor, Mr. Thomas Nevitt, thought so well of his Burwash wife, that he erected to her memory, not only a tablet in Burwash Church, but also a stately monument, as it is called in this memorandum, in the parish church of St. Benet, *alias* St. Benedict, Paul's Wharf, London; so that Burwash, if the church and monument still remain, is not without its memorial even in the great city.[1] Moreover, before Thomas May had died, and in the year after Mr. Nevitt's gift, Bateman's was built. Old Mr. Edwards (æt. 83), of Rye Green, tells me (1873) that when a boy he worked for Mr. Pattenden at Bateman's, and that Mr. Pattenden used to say that when Bateman's was built the men had a penny a day, and that the builders wanted to bate something off that, so they called the house Bateman's![2] The date of this house, 1634, we know by the stone over the door, and the date is nearly all that we do know. A Mr. Langham, who was buried here in 1652, was reputed a hundred years ago to have built the house; but this was doubted by Mr. Whitfield Curteis, who records the report. A Mr. John Britain, who lived at Bateman's, died and was buried here in 1707; and this apparently is all that we can find, without having other documents than those which are kept in the parish chest.[3] More will be known hereafter of the building

[1] The monument has perished. A friend of mine searched for it, and inquired of the sexton; but it was not to be found.

[2] "In 1610, when St. Paul's was being built, men's wages were 1d. per day."—Letter in *Times* of Tuesday, December 18, 1877; signed "A Lover of Justice and Fair Play."

[3] "Grandtwizle" Farm—I have often wondered what the meaning, if any, of this name could be. "Grand-teazel," a crop now grown on a farm near Lewes, for use in cloth manufacture, has been suggested; but in a book called "The Story of My Life," by Colonel

of some of our more modern houses, if, for instance, such a record as this is kept ; for on the 3rd of May, 1862, I laid the first brick of Mr. Gibbs' house. On the 18th of May, 1870, I laid the first brick of Miss Gould's house, the first stone of which was laid by Mrs. Wetherell on the 27th of the same month ; and, on the 24th of May, I laid the first stone of Mrs. Holland's house on Burwash Common.

The parchment which I now have in my hand is a terrier or list of the lands belonging to the glebe ; it bears date 1636, two years, that is, after the building of Bateman's, though, as it is only a copy of a document of that time in the Register Office at Lewes, we know nothing as to its own exact age. In 1636, however, William Langham, who was the reputed builder of Bateman's, was church-warden, and was, therefore, as I think I may say in the presence of other churchwardens, a gentleman of some consideration and importance. Whether in view of the troublous times that were coming or no, I cannot say, but we then needed, it seems, three churchwardens ; and one of them was Thomas Glyd, a descendant, no doubt, of the Thomas Glide who, in 1574, had to give the bond in the matter of the infringement of Ralph Hogge's right to the sole exportation of the Cast Iron Ordnance. It seems to me not improbable that the farm which we now call Glyd-dish, and which some would say stands for Gladwish, has the origin of its name somehow or other in Glyd ; it was called, perhaps, Glyd's, and then got to be Glyddish, I don't exactly know how, but possibly somehow, never-theless. At this date two out of the three sidesmen were Cruttendens, the other being Thomas Mitten.

There was now, too, another young man in the parish who was destined to leave a name behind him better known than the names of some of his fellow-parishioners. Edward Polhill, in after-life a theological writer of some

Meadows Taylor (Blackwood, 1877), I find Colonel Taylor mention-ing (vol. ii. p. 361) " the Cairns on *Twizell* Moor, Northumberland.' I wonder whether any meaning is assigned to this " *Twizell*."

repute, was born in this parish in 1617. He wrote several books, one of which, under the title of " A View of Some Divine Truths," was reprinted from the edition of 1678 as lately as seventeen years ago, and published by Thomas Ward and Co., Paternoster Row. A copy of it was given by a descendant of the author to the late Mr. Gould. Mr. Polhill was a friend of the ministers who, on the passing of the Act of Uniformity in 1662, would not conform, and were therefore ejected from their livings ; and amongst others of Thomas Goldham, the parson of Burwash, who for conscience' sake gave up the vicarage.[1]

Mr. Polhill greatly befriended also another good man, Mr. Joseph Bennett, son of Joseph Bennett, the Rector of Warbleton, who was born in 1629, and educated by his uncle, Thomas English, Esq., of Brightling, who sent him to St. John's College, Cambridge. When he returned to Sussex, he preached for a time in Burwash. He was presented to Brightling rectory in 1658 ; but in 1662, he, like Mr. Goldham, resigned his living rather than force his conscience, and lived quietly in Brightling for twenty years. He kept for a time a school, which, however, was broken up by the Plague in 1665. In later life he removed to Hastings, and though, by his peaceable and pious conversation he had conciliated the friendship of many who were greatly prejudiced against Dissenters, yet, before his removal to Hastings, some malicious people, without the least founda-tion, formed a design of accusing him of high treason. A testimonial, however, was procured for him by E. P. of Burwash— which " E. P." I take to stand for Edward Polhill—from a neighbour of his, who was as high as any man, which brought him off, and his enemies were ashamed of their doings. He died in 1707.

His son, Mr. Joseph Bennett, jun., was sent to school here in Burwash under Mr. Goldham. From Burwash he went to a higher school, kept by Mr. Charles Morton at Newington Green ; he became a preacher, and accepted a

[1] See also p. 44 of this volume.

lectureship under " good old Mr. W. Wickens," as he was called at Stoke Newington. From Stoke Newington he went to be assistant to Mr. Shower, of the Old Jewry Chapel, and there he laboured with satisfactory success till he died, in 1726. For the space of forty years he lived the valued friend of Edmund Calamy, and the doctor paid him a last mark of respect by improving his departure in a funeral sermon, so that the foundation of his education laid in Burwash had not been without results in after-life.

In our registers of the date of 1680 I find a Robert Glazier buried ; hence, perhaps, " Glazier's Forge." About this time I find several instances of entries stating that such and such a person was buried in linen, or without a certificate, and that the fine was inflicted according to law. I asked Mr. Philcox what this meant, and he referred me to an Act passed in 1678 (30 Charles II), by which it was enacted that for the encouragement of the woollen manufacture, and prevention of the exportation of money for the importing of linen, no corpse of any person should be buried in any shirt, shift, sheet, or shroud, or anything whatsoever made or mingled with flax, hemp, silk, hair, gold, or silver, or in any stuff or thing, other than what is made of sheep's wool only on pain of £5, and the clergyman was bound to require a certificate of the fact. In 1685 I find the entry of the burial of a Nathaniel Panton, a doctor of medicine, and on a piece of paper, in Mr. Whitfield Curteis' handwriting, I see written against Dr. Panton's name, " Jokes recorded." Now, this is very tantalizing, as we are not told what the jokes were, or where they are recorded. The good doctor may have been funny enough to have made a man laugh while he was having a tooth pulled out, and, alas ! all the fun is lost ; but so it is. Our churchyard may have mouldering in it the dust of a very Joe Miller, and we are none the merrier. Still, if we have lost Dr. Panton's jokes, I own that I have heard some things said in Burwash as good, perhaps, as his were.

*   *   *   *   *

But we must be getting on with our history, as we have a hundred and eighty-three more years to account for, and not much time to do it in. On the 6th of October, 1687, John Gutsole was buried, leaving a name behind him which the owners of Gutsole Farm have long tried to conceal in Goodsoal, or in some other way, but which I now boldly drag to light again in all its repulsive plainness, and say that Gutsole is Gutsole, and nothing else.

Between the years 1649 and 1674, owing to various causes, the Government had not attended much to the coinage of the country, and there was a great lack of small change, such as halfpence and farthings, so that traders, whose business was of any importance, and who dealt much with the poor, were obliged to issue on their own account tokens, as they were called, of small value. In 1669 we had a tradesman here of the name of Edward Austen, whose business was large enough to make it worth his while to issue these tokens for himself; his halfpenny had on it on one side a man dipping candles over the figure " E A C," which I interpret to mean Edward Austen, Chandler, and on the other side the words " of Burwash " and " his halfpenny." Of this Edward Austen I can learn nothing except that he had a son, Edward, baptized in Burwash Church on the 28th of November, 1679, which son Edward appears to have been one of the churchwardens in 1724, as may be seen by the bond which I hold in my hand—a bond given by one Samuel Jones, of Salehurst to the churchwardens and overseers of Burwash, by which he bound himself to forfeit to them £20 if he did not, in case of his son-in-law, William Gibbons (a Burwash man whom he wanted to live with him in Salehurst), becoming chargeable to the parish, pay over immediately to the aforesaid churchwardens and overseers of Burwash the sum of £10. The Burwash people, it seems, were unwilling that William Gibbons should spend his youthful days, as the bond says, in Salehurst, and then come back in his later days to Burwash; the Salehurst people were equally unwilling that a new family should come into their parish, with the chance of becoming chargeable to them. So they would not let poor Master Gibbons into Salehurst till the Burwash people had given a certificate that they would make good to Salehurst any charge brought upon Salehurst by William Gibbons or his family; and this certificate the Burwash people were equally unwilling to give till Samuel Jones, the father-in-law, had bound himself in £20 that he would at once pay over to them £10 on either his son-in-law or his children becoming chargeable to Burwash. On this bond being given, the certificate was granted, and William Gibbons was allowed to settle in Salehurst. A roundabout business certainly, but interesting as a specimen of poor-law customs. Calling on a Salehurst man and his wife the other day (March 14, 1871), who had just settled in Burwash, I was saying how much easier migration is now than it used to be; and I referred to this Gibbons and Jones transaction in 1724. In the course of my visit I happened to look at the iron fireback which they had brought with them from Salehurst, and which the man, Edwin French, said had been in his family many years; by a curious coincidence the date on it was 1724, the very year in which the bond of which I had been speaking was given. It is now in my possession.[1] In 1724, as I have already said, the name of Edward Austen—the son of Edward Austen, who issued the tokens—comes in as church-warden.

Churchwardens and overseers were in those days powerful officers, for on this tattered paper which I now produce is a list or memorandum of " the houshould goods of William Cruttenden, when it was seized by the churchwardens and overseers of the poore," in either January or February of the year 1697. Amongst the items we find several which we should look for in vain now, such as " one spinning

---

[1] At Bateman's there were some " dogs," or " brand-irons," or " and-irons," or " end-irons," bearing the date 1585. They were taken away by Mr. Stevenson when he left the farm, about 1873.

wheel," and " one new spinning wheel," and " three pewter
dishes." There was apparently no crockery, but there
was one dozen of trenchers or wooden platters, and one
iron skillet ; there were " foure chaires," two tables, and
one " forme," a warming-pan, a frying-pan, and a fire-pan,
" 4 barrells, 3 tubbs, and 4 keilers," on all of which rude
hands were laid. On March 20, 1871, I called on Mrs.
Cramp, of Daw's Farm, whose mother was a Cruttenden,
and she showed me a pewter dish, and three wooden
trenchers, such as those just mentioned. The pewter dish
is what we now call a hot-water plate, and the trenchers
are round, with a slight hollow in the middle for gravy.

At Platt's farmhouse is still a " boulter," or machine
with which farmers dressed the flour at their own houses,
the corn being simply ground at the mill.

In the year 1713 the Congregational chapel [1] at the
bottom of the village was built by the Mr. Edward Polhill
of whom we have spoken ; for on a pane of glass in one of
the windows of the chapel is, or was, written, " John
Baker, glazier ; this house of prayer was built in the year
of our Lord 1713."

As a Churchman, it is not without grief that I record
this pane, inasmuch as more zeal on the part of the Church
might have rendered the chapel unnecessary ; and yet in
1685 the Church had been alive to the wants of the congregation, for in the churchwardens' account of that year
I find paid to the carpenters, for building the gallery and
timbers, £18 10s. Whether building the new chapel had
anything to do with the still increased accommodation in
the church I do not know, but the last document of any age
which I have found is dated 1720, and is a subscription
list for building one of the galleries which used to be in
the church. The gallery was built by contract for £30.
Of this sum £13 17s. 6d. was raised by a tax of twopence
in the pound on the land in Burwash parish, the rest by

---

[1] In this chapel the celebrated Dr. Watts is said to have preached.
—MS., Redcross Street Library, London.

subscriptions. Mr. Jordan, the vicar, gave £1 1s.; Mr. John Cruttenden, £2 2s.; Mr. Henry Gouldsmith, £1 10s.; Mr. Edward Austen, sen., and Mr. Edward Austen, jun., of whom we have spoken before, £1 1s. each; Mr. Paul Gibbs, 10s. 6d.; and Mr. John Lawrence, singing-master, 5s.

I may here remark that last year (1870) the name of Cruttenden died out in the parish, after having existed, as we have seen, in more or less dignity, for several hundred years. The two last possessors of the name were poor John Cruttenden, whom we remember so well, and old Master Cruttenden, who lived and died at Daw's Farm, which Mr. Cramp now uses.

One hundred and fifty years ago we also had in the parish two families of the same names as two families who at the present time are a very great help and assistance to us, viz. Gibbs and Breach. Mr. Paul Gibbs, we have just seen, helped to build a gallery in the church, which I fancy Mr. Andrew Gibbs helped by his subscription to pull down when our church was restored; but of Mr. Breach's namesake I know nothing more than that Elizabeth, daughter of John and Elizabeth Breach, was baptized here in 1693, and that Mr. John Breach [1] was bold enough to go all the way to Chichester in 1734 to vote for Pelham and Butler, the two candidates for the county who, in Burwash at all events, were the popular ones. For reference to this poll, see S. A. C., xxiii. 75. Here, again, there is a dearth of history in the records of the parish, and it is a time during which I fear the parish was not improving. Smuggling was increasing rapidly on the Sussex coast, and Pevensey Bay, which we see from " Gingerbreads," or " Sea-View " as it is now called, was a favourite neighbourhood with the adventurers. For instance, one morn-

---

[1] Extract from Sussex Poll Book, 1734, sent me by the Rev. J. R. Munn, Vicar of Ashburnham : " At this election forty-three Burwash voters polled (though of them eight were non-resident), and amongst them we find William Shadwell, Gent., William Constable, Esq., and John Coney, Gent. In 1872 there were a hundred and twenty-six electors on the register."

ing in the month of December, 1745, there was a terrible alarm in London, owing to an express having arrived at the Duke of Newcastle's (one of the family, I imagine, of our Burwash Pelhams) the night before, with an account that the French were actually landed in Pevensey Bay. The duke went to the coast immediately, but before any steps could be taken in consequence of this news, a second express brought the duke word it was nothing more than a gang of smugglers that landed in the bay, and gave out the French were coming, on which the custom-house officer and many others fled, and left the smugglers literally a clear coast to bring all their run goods on shore, and to dispose of them in such a manner as should be best for their security (" Malmesbury Letters," vol. i. 23 : Bentley, 1870). Our parish lies right in the way of any communication between parts of the coast and Surrey and other inland places, so unfortunately we were much visited by smugglers, and not a little linked up with them. However, thank God, smuggling is pretty nearly over now. There are wiser laws, and the temptation is so much lessened by lowering the duties on spirits, that it is not worth men's while now to run the risks of breaking the law. We may go now into cottages without the thought that possibly tub-holes are concealed under our feet ; we may look at the floor without suspecting that, by the application of a sucker, a well-fitted brick would come up and reveal a world of spirits to our astonished eyes ; and we may pass along our roads by night or day without a chance of meeting a string of horses laden with contraband, and ridden by men prepared to shoot anyone who might interrupt them. We have not an excise officer in the place to shut his eyes at certain times, and to open them only when the danger was past, and the smugglers' thank-offering, in the shape of an anker of brandy, lay at the door. Our days are quieter and less exciting, perhaps, than these days of old, but I for one am well content that they should be so.

And yet, in the midst of all this lawlessness, a learned

scholar, divine, and poet came to live among us, who when he left the parish in 1792, on the death of a beloved sister, could say to a friend in Oxford (Lower's " Sussex Worthies," p. 167), " Dear Sir,—Having been expelled by calamity from my little paradise at Burwash, the world is all before me, and I am once more to choose my place of rest."   Mr. Hurdis, the writer of this letter, was curate of Burwash from 1786 to 1791.   He lived at " Fry's," and there wrote a poem called " The Village Curate," which secured its author an immediate reputation.   In 1788 " Fry's " was thus portayed to the world—

> " In yonder mansion . . . which scarce a mile
> From village tumult to the morning sun
> Turns its warm aspect, yet with blossoms hung
> Of cherry and of peach, lives happy still
> The reverend Alcanor. On a hill
> Halfway between the summit, and a brook
> Which idly wanders at its foot, it stands,
> And looks into the valley wood-besprent,
> That winds along below.
>   On the hill-top, behold
> The village steeple, rising from the midst
> Of many a rustic edifice ; 'tis all
> The pastor's care."

Of this poem, a brother-poet of still greater fame, William Cowper, writes, " Let genius, true genius, conceal itself where it may, we say of it, as the young man in Terence of his beautiful mistress, ' diu latere non potest '—it cannot long lie hid."   Some years ago, when I was curate of Downton, in Wiltshire, a woman, one of my then parishioners, gave me a piece of wood, which she told me was a piece of Mr. Cowper's oak tree at Olney, in Buckinghamshire, where he lived, and where she had been in service. I happen to have kept the wood, little thinking that in Burwash I should ever produce it as a sort of memorial of the great friend of Mr. Hurdis, the Burwash curate.

Soon after Mr. Hurdis left Burwash,[1] he was appointed Professor of Poetry in Oxford, and after his early death, in 1801, his widow published his poems. The Queen, of her own free will, offered to receive the dedication of them to her. No less than 1278 persons, if I have counted them correctly, gave their names as subscribers, and 1519 copies were subscribed for ; and in the preface to the poems, the name of Burwash was introduced to the royal family, and the reading public of England, as being the scene of the principal poem, with a credit which modern unbelievers, when they hear the sound of Burwash, only honour with a smile.

We now reach contemporary history, and really and truly I ought to stop my pen, and bring before you in the flesh men who could tell you their own experiences of the last seventy years in Burwash. Master John Hicks came to live in the parish in 1799, being then about sixteen years old. Mr. John Vigor, who is now, too, over eighty, has lived in Burwash all his life ; and either of them could, I am sure, detail to you the various changes which have taken place in the parish in that long time far more vividly than I can. Mr. Vigor, especially, could tell you of our fortnightly assemblies and card-parties at the " Rose and Crown," where the aristocracy of the parish and neighbourhood used to meet for cards and gossip. He could speak of neighbouring magistrates driving to our petty sessions—Mr. Newberry from Heathfield with four horses, Mr. Fuller of Rose Hill with four, Mr. Courthope with two,

[1] October 27, 1794, " A contest took place for the poetry professorship between Mr. Kett, of Trinity, who had preached the ' Bampton Lectures ' in 1790, and Mr. Hurdis, of Magdalen, the author of some pleasing but not first-rate poems, and a tragedy, entitled ' Sir Thomas More.' Hurdis had 201 votes ; Kett, 181. The first edition of Hurdis' poems was printed by himself and his sisters at their private press in the village of Cowley, near Oxford, where he resided. After his death, about 1808, another edition was published, with a very large subscription for copies, in aid of his sisters, who were in rather reduced circumstances."—Cox's " Recollections of Oxford " (Macmillan, 1868).

and Mr. Robert Hawes of Markly with two. John Hicks could tell you how, when he was overseer, he was able to lower the poor tax to 28s. in the pound, it having been as high as 28s. 10½d. ; and Mr. Vigor could bear him out by saying that about 1823 or 1824 he paid 24s. in the pound himself for three years.

Another parishioner [1] could tell you how when his grandfather was overseer he got into some trouble because he would not allow a labouring man pumps for his daughter to go to a dance in. He would allow the man half-boots for himself, but pumps for his daughter he would not allow.

Mr. Vigor could tell you how in 1814 he gave fourteen pence a pound for mutton, and how in 1822 he bought ten and a half stone of good mutton for a sovereign ; and yet this latter was the time when the poor rates alone were very often more than the rent. Other old people can tell you how they remember flour three shillings and fourpence a gallon ; and men now alive can recollect the time when there were eighty people employed by the parish on the Bough Farm—how one of the men picked up one day a dead robin, how they all took it into their heads to give this robin a public funeral, and how at the parish expense these eighty men spent two days in the business. Robert Watson, now alive (1881) in Burwash, aged about forty, unvaryingly affirms that when he was a child and living at Mottensden with his father, he and the rest of the family subsisted on absolutely and positively nothing but raw potatoes for about three weeks, at the end of which time his father and brother [2] sickened with typhus fever and

[1] Mr. J. B. Noakes, draper and grocer, Burwash.

[2] This is known to be the case, though the story always seemed to me an incredible one as regards the potatoes ; but in *The Times* of Tuesday, November 8, 1881, I find, under the head of " Disasters at Sea," that the crew of the Norwegian barque *Helme*, abandoned in the Atlantic on October 7, consisting of Captain Nanson and two men, were in great distress by reason of their provision having been spoilt by sea-water. " The only article of food upon which they subsisted being uncooked potatoes. In this condition they remained for eight days, when the Bremen barque *Olbero* hove in sight and came to their rescue."

died. Mrs. Lydia Luck can tell you how, when twelve years old, she worked a whole week for the parish on the Bough Farm and Gutsole Farm for the high wages of no money and find herself. Mr. Vigor could say, if he were here, how at one election he took seventy-two voters to Brighton on their way to poll at Chichester, and how " Jack Fuller " was elected for East Sussex after a twenty-one days' poll at Lewes. He could tell you something of the feelings with which we Burwash people used to watch the beacon on Brightling Hill night after night, which stood ready to be lighted in a moment should the French begin to land. Were old Mr. Dunk alive, who died hardly more than a year since, he could give you all the particulars as to when and where he was to drive the wagons loaded with the household goods, and the women and children of the west part of our parish, as soon as he saw the light ; and Mr. Vigor, as one of the body called " Sussex Guides," can tell us how he would have had to hurry away to Battle, and "from thence guide the army the nearest way he could to the enemy." He has told me how old Mr. Joel Newington's father, being called upon suddenly for a toast or sentiment at a party of friends, gave extempore the following more patriotic than poetic effusion—

> " May Buonaparte,
>   With all my heart,
> Land in Pevensey Level ;
>   We'll meet him there
>   And fight him secure [? square],
> And drive him to the devil."

All this and plenty more there are men amongst us able to remember. And when we compare those times with these, we may, I think, be somewhat reconciled to the loss of the good old days, when children were told to lie still or else " Boney " would have them, and were sent to bed with the strictest orders that if the gentlemen (that is, the smugglers) came through the streets they were not to look out of the window ; when, as John Hicks remembers, one high-road to Lewes was fagoted near Morris town in Heathfield ; and when, as one of the three men who first began "the mobbing" in Burwash told me, hundreds of men out of work would seize a landlord or a parson almost bodily, and make him promise to lower his rent or his tithes. This, I believe, they did to Dr. Totty, Rector of Etchingham, whom they took to Hurst Green and there made him promise what they liked. I dare say that there are, too, some amongst us who can remember the issuing of the following notice, which in these small-pox days [1] is not uninteresting, and which seems to have been put forth about the beginning [2] of the century, and which Mr. J. Fleming has found in an old book of his father's : "Thomas Baldock, surgeon at Burwash in Sussex, begs leave to inform the public that he attends on people desirous of having the small-pox by inoculation, either at their own houses, or accommodates them with all necessaries in houses he has provided for that purpose for three weeks after inoculation, at one and a half, two, or three guineas per person. He engages to attend them in the distemper with the utmost care and fidelity, pursuing the new and most approved method now practised." At any rate, Mr. Taylor well remembers Mr. Frank Russell often telling him how, when he was a lad, he worked hard and earned a guinea that he might have the small-pox. The house on Holton Farm, then in Mr. Baldock's possession, was a "pest-house," or house for persons having small-pox. About 1825 Ben Wood watched the grave of Richard Pilbeam, son of Edward and Deb. Pilbeam, to prevent the body being snatched for the doctor. This was done for nearly a month. Old Tom Wood, ostler at the "Rose and Crown," also watched for some of the Cane family. No ; I again, for one, am glad these good old days are

[1] About this time (1871) there were a few cases of small-pox in Burwash.

[2] Or earlier than this, as Mr. Baldock died in 1802.

gone; they are all very well to talk about or to lecture about, but, as far as I can see, they are good for nothing else except to make us thankful for the somewhat better days we have got.

There is a common opinion among us that men of the present generation in Burwash are not as strong as men of fifty years ago. To-day (March 22, 1871) I was speaking to old Master Weeks, carter to Mr. Simes, and was asking him as to the truth of a feat of strength which I had heard attributed to him. He assured me that it was absolutely true that when he was a young man, fifty years ago and more, a wagon-load of wheat which he was taking to the mill (Relfe's mill) tilted over by accident into a pond, and that he there and then jumped in and fetched out one by one the fifteen sacks of wheat, and this so quickly that they did not get wet enough to need drying before they were ground. Each sack contained four bushels of wheat, and weighed at least two hundred and forty pounds, and the old man said that at the time he thought nothing of what he had done.

I have also within the last few days been told of a man of forty or fifty years ago, known by the nickname of " Rudy-boy," who is reported to have carried a pair of six-inch wheels on his shoulder across a fallow field, and also to have lain on his back on the ground under a wagon with a thousand of bricks in it, and to have lifted it off the ground with his feet !

It is the fashion to speak of East Sussex children as dull and stupid, and of the men in the same way. If the allegation be true, I have often said that much, surely, is owing to the conditions of Sussex labourers' life.[1] The

[1] In reference to this theory, I made the following extract out of M. Taine's " History of English Literature," vol. i. p. 24 (Edmondston and Douglas, Edinburgh, 1871) : " The sap of this humid country [Holland], thick and potent, circulates in man as in the plants, and by its respiration, its nutrition, the secretions and habits which it generates, affects his faculties and his frame." Also, " We can yet assert that the profound differences which are manifest

BURWASH—VILLAGE STREET, LOOKING EAST

boys begin as carter-boys, and have to drag their heavy boots through clay fields and heavy lanes day after day; they grow up on clay—quick bodily movement is always impossible, and in time the body affects the mind, and all is slow together; and the children inherit their parents' nature.

As in after-days [1] the original and possibly remote causes of any social or political movements are specially interesting, I here record the steps by which the great change in the fortunes of Burwash Common took place, and gladly acknowledge that that change is, humanly speaking, due originally to the respect and esteem which worth and excellence in any rank of life secure for their possessors. In or about the year 1857, Mr. William Smith, formerly house-steward in the service of Lord Dartmouth, and whose wife had been a confidential servant in the family of Lord Dunmore—then living at Eastbourne—purchased the small property at Burwash Common called Buckle's Farm. Mr. Smith had lived some years previously in the village of Rusper in another part of the county—in which village Mr. Francis Trower and his family also lived. Mr. Trower having removed to London, and wanting at times to send his young children into the country, sent them for several years in the summer to Mr. and Mrs. Smith at Burwash Common. Having been himself to see them there, he was struck with the beauty of the country, and when his sisters, the Misses Trower, were anxious to leave Redhill, where they were residing, he suggested to them the purchase of Buckle's Farm, now called Hollyhurst, which Mr. Smith was anxious to sell. Soon after their settlement at Hollyhurst, the Misses Trower began the various agencies which by God's blessing are now doing so much good.

between the German race on the one side, and the Greek and Latin on the other, arise for the most part from the difference between the countries in which they are settled."

[1] "Curiosity with reference to origin is, for various reasons, the most marked element among modern scientific tendencies."—J. Morley, "On Compromise" (Chapman and Hall, 1874).

II

They opened a school, and were mainly instrumental in getting the present church built. Had there been no church, the Honourable Mrs. Holland would not, so we understand, have settled at Oakdown, and another element of help would have been lost ; and thus to the circumstance of Mr. F. Trower's thinking well enough of Mr. and Mrs. Smith to send his children to stay with them, I trace the reformation of one of the wildest districts in Sussex.

When the time comes for the history of Burwash in the nineteenth century to be written, we shall find a place given in it to Mr. James Ellis, father of the present J. Ellis, Esq., of Barming, who was, I believe, the largest hop-grower in England, growing nearly a thousand acres of hops, and who was born in Burwash. A large place will be given to the late Rev. Joseph Gould, a true benefactor to the parish, of which he had spiritual charge for many years [1] ; a place also to the Rev. Ernest Hawkins, whose first curacy was under Mr. Gould, and who became afterwards well known to all Churchmen as the able secretary of the S.P.G., and who died a Canon of Westminster ; to the Misses Trower, the regenerators, if we may say so, of Burwash Common ; and we trust to not a few more who will leave their mark on the parish for good.

[1] The Rev. Joseph Gould, M.A., of Balliol College, Oxford, Prebendary of Chichester and Rural Dean, was curate in charge of Burwash from 1824 to 1840, and Rector and Vicar of Burwash from 1840 to October 6, 1866.

EXTRACTS FROM REGISTERS, CHURCH-WARDENS' ACCOUNTS, ETC.

IN 1711 the assessment was £843, and the poor tax, at
1s. in the £, was £83 13s.

Allowed by G. Courthope (sic).

      ,,   J. Frewin.

Another 6d. rate carried them through the year—

£41 6s. 0d.

_____

For the year £124 19s. 0d.

Poor people at this date were called " Goodman," as
Goodman Blackford ; " Goody," as Goody Moate.

" July, 1712. Paid Widow Hoash for to buy her a
porridge pott and keller 02. 00." So that oatmeal was
then, we may suppose, a common form of food ; or
porridge may have been then, as it is now, flour boiled
thick.

About the bells, see churchwardens' account, 1714.

Entries in register were not always very dignified—

" Sepulturae 1596–7 : Ould Mother Cruttenden, Feb. 7."

Odd names—

Margery Dawe, buried July 19, 1608. (" See-saw,
Margery Dawe." Old rhyme.)

Doegood Fuller, married Ap. 27, 1620.

Maria Cryer, married Nov. 29, 1686.

Thomas Lavender and Francisca Thunder, married
1699.

Faintnot Owen, d. of Thomas Owen, bapt. Mar. 9,
1622.

Obedience Hunt, married Jan. 28, 1661.

Grantwizle.   So spelt, 1650.

Thankful Ticehurst, married May 15, 1662.

Susanna, d. of John Breach, bapt. Jan. 19, 1661.

Elizabeth Cason—generosa—died Feb. 28, 1679.

Paul Gibbs, s. of Paul and Maria Gibbs, bapt. Aug. 19, 1686.

Domina Elizabeth Webb, buried Sept. 12, 1695.

Thomas Dike—generosus—buried Ap. 24, 1693.

In 1612 there were fifty-nine burials in Burwash Church-yard.

First entry of Burialles and not Sepulturae, 1621.

  „   „   Marriages and not Matrimonia, 1623.

Name Polhill first appears in Baptisms Anno Dom. 1622—

Edward Polhill sonne of Edward Polhill, Sept. 29.

Thomas Polhill sonne of Thomas Polhill, Oct. 6.

Jan. 1675. A tax made by the churchwardens and other inhabitants of the parish of Burwash for the reparoñ on the Church there at the rate of ob : ½ L^{li} per £—

Fishers	rated at	£34	
Grandtwisle	,,	40	
Glydwish	,,	5	
& for the wood . . .	,,	6	
The Park	,,	22	
Platts	,,	10	
Frenches	,,	85	10s.
Brownings	,,	18	

&c. &c.

Total of tax at a halfpenny in the pound, £4 11s. 2¾d., representing a ratable value of £2189 10s., but in 1706 the ratable value had sunk to £1677 10s.

1873. Ratable value £9778. At a halfpenny in the pound, £20 7s. 5d.

1675. P^d for watching the Church when
    Mr. Cason was buried ..   ..
    Expended in numbering ye people   1s. 6d.

| 1676. | Washing the surplice three times | 3s. | |
| 1873. | ,,   ,,   ,, | 3s. | |

A singular instance of fixity of prices.

1676.	P^d for washing the Cloak for the Communion Table and scouring the cupps .. .. .. £	02	00
	P^d for killing a fox	01	00
1678.	For ringing the eight o'clock bell curfew and keeping the clock..	01 00	00
	Paid for an hour glasse for Mr. Webb	00 00	08
1680.	Mr. Constable rated for Turzies at £52		
1682.	Paid for an houre glasse	00 00	08
1684.	Paid Goodman Avory for a fox by him taken	00 01	00
	Oct. 2. Item. Half a pint of sack to drink while the presentments were writing	00 00	06
1686.	Given to 4 gentlemen passengers	00 00	06
	Given Mr. Polhill's boy for three hedgehogs		6
	Doctor Paul Gibbs—Church tax		6
1690.	Paid for a horse's journey to Hastings	1	6
1692.	Paid for Mr. Webb's (the Vicar) dinner at the Visitation	2	0
1693.	Given to one driven out of Ireland		6
	Given a woman with a pass with the king's broad seal	1	0

APPENDIX

BY special permission, we are accorded the privilege of publishing the two following letters. They appeared originally in a Sussex local paper in or about the year 1870, and are a unique and inimitable example of the now almost obsolete Sussex dialect.

They were written by the Revd. William Douglas Parish (b. 1833–d. 1904), Vicar of Selmeston and Alciston, county of Sussex, 1863–1904—Chancellor of Chichester Cathedral, 1877–1900. Author of " The Domesday Book in relation to the County of Sussex," 1886, and of the " Dictionary of the Sussex Dialect," 1875, to which Mr. Coker Egerton made some valuable contributions.

ACCOUNT OF THE WEDDING OF —— AT —— SUSSEX

BY A LABOURER OF THE PARISH

Hond. Sir,—

I takes the libbaty to write these few lines hopping they will leave you quite well as they finds me at present, to tell you all 'bout dis here gurt weddin and todo up at Furrel, for I thort as you'd like to have a pertickler and kract account ont all, to put into de peaper a Saddaday.

'Twas one of my lord's grandarters as was to be married, but I can't spell her name nohows in de wurreld.

Dey do say as she be a gurt favrite of my lord's and no wonder nother, for she's a honaccountable plessan peart young laddy surelye, and tarks to any one jes as free, and

as for the rheumatticks!! Lar bless ye! 'Twould make
ye forgit ye'ed ever had 'em to hear her larf.

Wall, dere was to be over three hunderd people had in
to dinner up at the ridin' school; 'twas de cheldern, and
de laybrers, and all as was 'bove sixty yeeres of age.

So 'twas over a wick agoo, de passon he comed down
our house, and ast me whedder I was 'bove sixty yeeres of
age.

"Wall, sir," I sez, "I doan't jesly know how old I be,
but I noos I be 'bove sixty yeeres of age, for ye see I went
to work when I was somewheres 'bout nine yeeres old (dat
was in old Mus Ridge's time) and I kep on till I was sum-
wheres 'bout fower and twenty, and den a young woman
got me into trouble, and I was force to goo away to sea,
but I diddun hold to that not much 'bove six or seven yeeres,
and den I come home and got drawed for de meleshia and
sarved ten yeeres, and den volunteered for a sodger and
sarved my time fefteen yeeres, and den I come back to
de farm, and dere I've worked for fower and forty yeer,
till I got quite entirely eat up wid de rheumatticks, and
now I ain't done naun for dese las' ten yeeres, and sometimes dey be better dan what dey be othersome. So I
noos I be 'bove sixty yeeres of age.

But, howsomever, I must be gittin on, for de women-
folk 'ul be wantin to read all 'bout dis weddin.

And, fuss of all, I mus tell you dat I've had a very gurt
misfortin, all through along on account of losin a hog: and
she jes wos a purty hog tew. I bought her when she warn't
but seven wicks old, off old Master Chawbery, time he
lived down de street, up agin the church.

Supprisin gurt hog she growed tew be sure!

Dere was a man come from Uckful one day and looked
at her; and dere was a man from Lunnun, he see her, and
dey both allowed as dey'd never seed sich a hog all dere
lives. And she hadn't had naun but three bushels of
pollard nother.

Ah, you'd have been pleased to see her, I know. Dere

was a many used to come down of a Sunday and looked at her; and old Master Chawbery and me, we'ev stood over de poun whiles people was in church, and rackoned her up and looked her over for hours together; and we both guv it in as she wouldn'd weigh no less than seventy stun.

And she hadn'd had naun but three bushels of pollard nother.

Wall, one marnin, 'bout three wicks agoo ('twas of a Saddaday) I was gwine ra-ound by de pa-ound, and I looks over, and dere was de hog, seemingly 'bout as common, and pensley I looks round agun, and dere she was all stratched out and gaspin for breath.

So I goos indoors and ses, "Mestress," I ses, "de hog be countable ornary."

"Wall," ses she, "dere aint no call for yew to come spannelin' 'bout my clean ketchen naun de moor for dat," she ses.

"Ah," ses I, "but she be countable bad, mestress," I ses, "and I dunno but what she be gwine to die."

"Massy pon me," ses she, "gwine to die! Never! Surelye."

"Yew come ra'ound and look at her, den," I ses.

Soon as ever she seen her, she ses to me, she ses, "Why doant ye give her somethin," she ses, "standin here!"

So I got down a gurt bottle of stuff what I had from de doctor time my leg was so bad, and took and mixed it in with some skim-milk and a liddle pollard and give it her, jes lew warm.

But it didn't seem as she was anyways de better for it, and all nex day she kep on getting wus, and she died de Monday night as she was took de Saddaday. And it seemed jes a though 'twas to be, for naun as we could give her didn't do her no good whatsumdever.

Dere was a dunnamany people come and looked at her. And we had her opened, and Master Chawbery he allowed as she was took wid de information.

No more at present ; but I thought I'd write and tell ye all 'bout our gurt doins, for de women folks moast always likes to read 'bout a weddin.

Yours spackfully,
JOHN HOGPOUND.

POSCRIP.—Come to think ont and rackont up, I dunno as she did have three bushels pollard, not by pert nigh half a gallon.

JOHN HOGPOUND'S ACCOUNT OF THE SHAH

HOND SIR,—

I've been a gwine to write tyeu frverslong 'bout dis 'ere Shah. Master Chawbery he comes in about a wick agoo, and he says to me, he says, " Deres a hem set out over dis here Shah, Master Hogpound—I rackon you'll be for gwine up to Lunnon jes for to look em over shaant ye ? " ses he.

" Wall," I says, " I dunno but what I will,"—and cardenly I goos arf Monday morning fustrain,—Ah, it jes was a purty sight, I can tell ye,— purtiest sight ever I see, and I wants ye to putt it in de peaper.

Soonsever I gets into de train dere was a chep set aside of me, and he says to me, says he, (knowed me he did,) " Wall, Master Hogpound," he says, " where be you a gwine smarnin ? " " Wall," I says, " I be a gwine up to Lunnon," says I, " to see dis here Prooshun."

" Prooshun ? " saysee—" what Prooshun ? "

" Why dis here Shah," I says, " as deres so much tark-about," Jes did laugh he did. " Darnel ! " he says, " why he beant a Prooshun, Master Hogpound,—he's a Persian he is."

" Wall," I says, " 'tis all one, Prooshuns and Persians, some calls 'em Prershuns and some calls 'em Prooshuns, and Master Chawbery," I says, " he allways calls 'em Prooshuns, and he's a marn as has moved about purty much all over de wurreld, he has,—he's been down into Kent and all manner ! And he worked above two years along 'ud a marn as come up out of Hampsheer, and Master Chawbery he's giv it in as dis here Shah's a Prooshun, and I'll be bound he aint fur out nither."

Wall, he couldn't say naun agin that ye see, so he didn't say no more about de Persians, and we kep on a tarkin about de weather and one thing and tother till a young man came and opened de doors and asks for de tickuts, "Tickuts," he says, so dey all helps him to dere tickuts, and prensley he asks me for my tickut, and darnell if I could find me tickut anyhows in de wurreld.

Dere was a farming man sat tother side, and he says, "Preps tis fell under de seat," he says : so we looked under de seat, but she warn't there, and de chep he keeps on all de time "Tickuts," he says, "I wants your tickut."

"Ca'ant find her," I says.

"Wall, den," he says, "if you airn't got no tickut you'll have to pay de hexcess."

"What's that ? " says I. "Sixanfopence," says he.

"Den I won't pay no sich money," I says.

"Ah, we'll see about that prensley," he says, and he goos and tarks to de Inspactor. So whiles he was gone I looks everywheres, I goos down on my handsneeze and sarched all over de flower, I took off my hat, and shoke out my pockutankercher, and all manner,—dunno when I've been so much put out, not since I lost dat gurt hog.

So de Spacter comes, and he says "Well, my friend," he says, "lost your tickut, have yer ? "

"Yessir," I says : "Well, you'll have to pay," he says, "but if your station master knows you've took a tickut, you'll be able to get the money back by writing to de Sackitry."

"Wall, when he tarked so civil and spackful-like, and said as how I should have de money give back to me, I putts my harnd into my pockut, to fetch out my money purse, and soonsever I putts my harnd into my pockut dere was de tickut. Be darnell if she warnt in my old pockut all de whole time !

So nex time as any of dese here Shahs comes over, and you goos to Lunnon or anywheres to see 'em, and anyone asks for your tickut, you make sure and sarch your pockuts afore you gives in that she's lost.

Yours spackfly,
JOHN HOGPOUND.

POSCRIPT.—'Twas my traowsiers pockut.

Printed in Great Britain by Butler & Tanner Ltd., *Frome and London*